Seismic Shifts...
When God Has Moved On

Allious Gee

Copyright © 2019 by Allious Gee
Published by Allious Gee
Durham, NC

All rights reserved. No part of this publication may be reproduced, distributed, or transmitted in any form or by any means, including photocopying, recording, or other electronic or mechanical methods, without the prior written permission of the publisher, except in the case of brief quotations embodied in critical reviews and certain other noncommercial uses permitted by copyright law.

Start Write Team:
Cover Design & Project Manager: Rainah Davis
Lead Editor: Tequilla Davis
Assistant Editors: Gerald Simmons / Cherie Graham
Layout Design: Erica Smith

ISBN-13: 978-0-9994626-2-1

Dedication

This book is dedicated to my dear wife Debby without whom I dare say the seasons of change in my life would not have gone so smoothly. We have had some wonderful years together. Thank you for your prayers, companionship and invaluable support.

Contents

PREFACE 1

CHAPTER 1 STRIPPED: My Story 3

CHAPTER 2 The Sin of Missing God 13

CHAPTER 3 When God Has Moved On 23

CHAPTER 4 An Invitation to a Revelation 33

CHAPTER 5 Two Revelations
                       that Changed Everything 43

CHAPTER 6 What Happened to My Joy 53

CHAPTER 7 Peter's Prejudice 77

CHAPTER 8 Changing What God Hates 83

CHAPTER 9 Changed to Reign 95

CHAPTER 10 Abandoning Ineffective Prayers 101

CHAPTER 11 Living Where God Was 109

CHAPTER 12 When Your Anointing Changes 121

CONCLUSION The Final Shift 127

PREFACE

Anyone seriously planning to walk with God cannot afford to be complacent, not for a moment. Just when we become confident that we can relax into autopilot, God shifts. When He does, we must be prepared for total change. Walking with God requires that we keep our bags packed. He has a reputation of being unchangeable, but as far as we know, He's the only entity in this entire universe that is. Everything else around Him is experiencing continuous transformation. Every moment the world changes in politics, education and technology, as well as in the social and cultural arenas. Accordingly, the physical world is also undergoing an alarming metamorphosis. Experts continually warn us of disturbing changes in weather patterns, geological shifts and of an unrelenting environmental decline. News reporters appear to be engaged in a feverish competition for who can shock our collective mindsets the most with discoveries of new forms of highly contagious incurable diseases, contradictory nutrition revelations and drug company cover-ups. Keeping up with these changes is not only key to our well-being, but also our very survival. The ability to adapt and improve is a necessary survival skill. Everyone from the entrepreneur to the educator is working hard to stay abreast of the numerous changes occurring so rapidly. However, in the midst of such changes, one entity has earned high marks for ignoring and resisting the necessity to change- the Church. Its resistance to change is worn as a badge of honor and commendation. To this very day, church leaders continue to pride themselves on just how fiercely they can cling to *the old landmark.* But this bent for maintaining the status quo is becoming costly. It assures that, for years to come, church policies and practices will remain largely irrelevant to society.

CHAPTER 1
STRIPPED: MY STORY

After eighteen years as pastor of a denominational church in Omaha, Nebraska, I was excited about the prospect of moving back to eastern Long Island. I left New York a young man in my twenties, and now at age forty-four, I felt God was directing me to return. By no means had I accomplished what I started out to do. I had envisioned leading a great work and saving many souls. That's not to say that each person saved was not indeed a miracle, but I thought that by now, there would have been many more. I felt a sense of regret about that, but in my spirit, I sensed a profound change. God had given me a new assignment in a new venue. But what I had just endured in Omaha, the town I had been sent to conquer for the kingdom, had so drastically changed me I knew nothing could ever be the same again.

In 1976, I arrived in Omaha fresh from ordination at our San Francisco convention. My new assignment was to spread the gospel and the outreach of our Apostolic denomination into the Midwest. This was what we called a *barren area* because we had no churches in that part of the country. This was also a progressive new vision by our Presiding Bishop to send young pastors into new areas to start churches with the eventual goal of increasing the denomination by 100 churches. It was an ambitious goal, but we young ministers felt energized to be a part of denominational history in the making. I was to secure a place to live, find employment and make new friends in preparation for starting the new work. As a single man, this was fairly easy to accomplish and in no time I had an apartment and was working. I was able, after approximately a year had elapsed, to find an affordable storefront building for a church, canvas the neighborhood, and kick off the first of many services in the new Faith Deliverance Church.

Prior to this ministry assignment, I had never even thought of Omaha. But gradually, as I put my heart into the work of ministry, I grew to appreciate and love the people. They were no different than any I had encountered in my early ministry in New York. Unaffected by the pace and the problems of the East and West coast cities, the people of Omaha were quite proud of having their own distinct identity. It was a town of people with strong family values and even stronger church loyalties. I found the religious boundaries between denominations, especially between the competing Apostolic and Pentecostals, to be both oppressive and confining.

Apostolics in this town declared Pentecostals *unsaved* because of baptism differences. Interdenominational fellowship was the exception and not the rule. It appeared that the more similar and closely aligned the beliefs of each group, the more pronounced the lines of separation. Disagreementstemming from the core beliefs on how an individual becomes *saved* festered at the root of these divisions. And, although there was much preaching of salvation and Heaven, territorial conflicts and church rivalries were a constant reminder of past arguments that were never reconciled.

The minority community was mostly comprised of scores of families whose relatives had migrated from the South to take advantage of the many job opportunities generated mainly by the utility companies, agricultural enterprises and meat packing plants. Mutual of Omaha was known worldwide and a major employer. And with the Union Pacific railroad system having the major share in the interstate shipping of livestock, grain and beef, jobs were plentiful. In addition, the nearby presence of Offutt Air Force Base, which housed the Strategic Air Command, also attracted military families into the area who remained and raised their families.

Omaha grew and developed into a sizeable town that, for the most part, provided its people the opportunities to make a good living. It has always had a reputation for being a great place to raise a family. It was in the setting of this hospitable mid-western town that God chose to turn my world upside down. My expectations were high that He would help me establish a growing, vibrant church full of people who loved the Lord and His work. Instead, God took the time, the years, to force me to face the pain of my own prejudices, shortcomings and narrow mindedness.

For a short time, I attended the largest apostolic church in Omaha. Having come from a church membership of 2,500, this was quite a culture shock. With a membership of approximately three hundred, it was huge compared to any other church in the denomination in Omaha. The clean, well-kept exterior and standing room only appearance of its crammed parking lot on Sunday mornings made it appear to be a great place to worship. The first time I heard the choir sing, I was hooked. From the musicians to the three-part harmonious blending of the singers' voices, the sound was electrifying. I was both moved and inspired. People were so friendly to visitors as they proudly extended the invitation for me to join.

At the time, I was the new saved single man in church. For a while that made me the center of attention. Invitations came regularly to come over for dinner, which I readily accepted. I was never disappointed because the food was always great and being welcomed into a family atmosphere made my periods of loneliness bearable.

Although I had no interest in developing any relationships with their eligible daughters beyond friendship, I was so impressed with the friendliness I experienced in their homes. I felt satisfied that I was following the instructions I received from the Presider before leaving New York to *make friends* upon my arrival. However, as a soon to be pastor, the reception I received from the pulpit was a different story. Convinced that I was there to steal his members, the pastor set about to make sure that would never happen on his watch. It was then that uncomplimentary rumors about me began circulating.

From that time onward, I sensed that I was being watched. It seemed like my every move was known. If I was seen with men, I was labeled a homosexual. If I was seen with women, I was a womanizer. On occasion, I also somehow became part of the pastor's Sunday sermon. I remember one sermon in particular which was quite scriptural in content until the pastor veered off with a left-handed comment that, "There are those who have been sent from the East and have come to take members to start a church." The comment came from left field and jerked me out of my daze. I knew I had told no one of my plans, but didn't know that someone, a relative of a member of my home church, thinking he would be helpful, had called him and told him of a young man coming to Omaha to start a church. Because I had no intention of taking even one member, I didn't think he was referring to me. I was so naive. I experienced open ridicule from him regarding my church affiliation.

He preached a gospel that convinced his members that they were the only ones going to Heaven in Omaha. They held that belief because of what they considered to be their deeper understanding of the scriptures on baptism and on the *oneness* of God (which totally rejects the concept of a trinity). They felt it was their duty to protect the tenets of the faith by exposing and opposing all who would dare to question or compromise. They viewed themselves as the only ones preaching the truth. So, just being seen attending a church of another denomination was interpreted that you were in fellowship with darkness. If the pastor got wind of it, you were in for an open rebuke. It was hard to believe that mature adults would indulge in such pettiness. As a result, the church social climate had all the makings of a small town gossip network with people secretly reporting to the pastor on the activities of others and rumors going back and forth between the members. Then on Sunday, the pastor would preach on things so private, we would all feel mortified for the one publicly disgraced. Saints meetings were regularly called to point out evildoers from the pulpit and to enforce church discipline. This served two practical purposes.

First, it kept everyone in line through fear of public humiliation. Secondly, it discouraged anyone from committing *reportable* sins. I classified them this way because of what I considered by far the most manipulative doctrine inflicted upon the members, the concept of confession. This teaching, more than any other, gave the pastor unlimited access to very private matters and ultimate control over their lives. Their doctrine decreed that whenever they sinned, they were immediately separated from God. God, no matter how sincere, would not hear any prayer from that point on. Of necessity, they, therefore, must contact a holy man (the pastor) and confess in order to be reconnected to God. Unless and until that was done, they believed that God would not hear them. Each of them was indoctrinated to believe that this was required. To be subjected to such obvious and outrageous coercion should have given even the most committed member cause to question its scriptural validity. But none questioned. It was accepted without a struggle. Desperate to maintain contact with God, the members, like sheep, would make that all-important call to confess. He alone was to be contacted to confess their wrongdoings or risk total estrangement from God. Such control evolved into total iron-fisted subjugation.

Born and raised a free spirit who frequently attended other churches and services, I became a prime target for his pulpit expose. I wasn't aware of it at the time, but there was a divine purpose for my exposure to this kind of abuse of authority, which would inflict inside me deep penetrating wounds that only God would be able to heal. To my total surprise, God was preparing to administer to me the most painful rebuke of my saved life, using this whole ordeal as his rod of correction. Through their mistreatment, I was forced to experience my own brand of insensitive treatment of others. I began to see how self-centered and arrogant I had been with people of other denominations that I considered in error. In the eyes of this church, I was condemned to hell for something as minor as my *natural* hairstyle. Surprisingly though, these people were very sweet and accommodating if you belonged to their church. But if you lived in Omaha and weren't a member of their congregation, you were considered either in error or lost.

Why was I there? Strangely enough, their beliefs were not too far from mine. Through that similarity alone God had driven home His point. To have any connection with that kind of religious bigotry and abuse was a serious indictment of my life. I thought I was sent to Omaha to save and to teach others. That was, to my knowledge, my initial assignment. But God was dealing with me as a father to a misguided son with one thing in mind, correction. How humbling it was for me to set out to instruct others to find myself a mere student in God's classroom of chastisement and correction. But, without giving me an explanation or any time to catch my breath, He set about to straighten out my thinking. I had developed a tendency to rely on my father in the gospel, the

Presider, when things got too tough to handle. He was a strong leader and well respected, which he earned by an unequaled work ethic and many noteworthy accomplishments. I respected his time too much to call for just anything. But, on one occasion, I had just been publicly attacked in the sermon of the pastor I mentioned above. He spoke of the founder of my denomination as if he was a hypocrite and a fool. He said in jest, "Bishop Dawson (not his name) preached against women preachers and turned around and married one." There was a burst of laughter followed by, "I don't understand that. That was Al Gee's founder."

I was devastated. No one had ever mentioned any of the accusations he was making. He even called out my name this time as the disciple of a hypocrite. I couldn't wait to get out of there to rush to a phone to ask, "Is there any truth to these allegations?" It took me a while to get through by phone. With wounded feelings and utter humiliation, I told Bishop what was said. And before I could get the question out, he cut me off with, "Son, I'm in a meeting." That was all. No set up of a future appointment to call. No empathy for my plight. Nothing more. Apparently, I had interrupted something important, much more important than my whole world that was being dismantled by this spiritual bully. After that, I made up my mind never to call again for help, and I didn't.

On virtually everything I had learned in ministry, from our strict stand against second marriages to female preachers, to our very beliefs about when a person is actually *saved*, God began to change my thinking. I responded by resisting His arguments with the scriptures I knew and with my limited understanding of them, which was always along denominational lines. But, one by one, He proved my thinking to be narrow-minded and out of touch with His will for His people.

CHAPTER 2
THE SIN OF MISSING GOD

It's absurd for Christians to be fighting an enemy who is equipped with the latest weaponry while we yet are using what is equivalent to bows, arrows and spears. Any army entering into battle with such a disadvantage cannot seriously expect victory. In ancient history, arrows, swords and spears were fearsome weapons but going into a battle armed with such now is suicide. That, however, is exactly what Christians are doing. We are being defeated by a severe lack of proper equipping.

Paul admonished believers to *put on the whole armor of God*. The implication is that the full armor is already available, but too many fail to put it on. Some are using obsolete weapons and waging war with outdated strategies. Battles lost, which should have been won in areas of health, finances, relationships, etc., continue to indicate a serious mismatch against us. We continue to be like sheep for the slaughter. To this kind of thinking, Paul said emphatically, "No, we're more than conquérors." What's the problem then? In spite of the fact that the most effective weapons have been available to us for some time, we missed God when it was time for change.

Change is a vital part of walking with God. When He updates, shifts or changes direction we must adapt. But many in the church have failed miserably at this. In their denominational pride and arrogance, they have become change resistant, forcing their membership into lives of defeat. Not because they're not well intended, but because they were unprepared for the fact that God changes. Neither in character nor integrity, but in methods, phases and seasons. We are continuing to commit the sin of being out of step with God. We are much too happy with being where God was, and much too content working to revive what God is finished with.

OUT OF TOUCH WITH GOD

While there is no such sin specifically called the sin of being out of touch with God, omission of certain critical things will ultimately lead us there. The solution is in two parts. The unread Bible that gathers dust on the shelf has the majority of the answers we need. We need to start seriously reading it. The other part is to begin striving aggressively to stay current with God's changes. God is a God on the move. He seems to have a penchant for new things, i.e., new creation, new birth, new covenant, new Heaven, new earth, etc. Some plans, purposes and pursuits can immediately become old when

God moves. One of the lessons we must know about Him is that He is constantly on the move and will at times change His focus and His direction. And no matter how involved and invested we are at the time of His shift, we must make the shift with Him. If not, the very victory we seek will be out of reach. We must deal with a God who changes. Wait a minute! Doesn't God state, "I am the Lord I change not." Yes, that is true. His character does not change, but He declares, "I will do a new thing."

FAILED PLANS AND MEDIOCRE RESULTS

If you have failed miserably while trying desperately to make your ministry plans work, you may see value in this book. The problem you've encountered may be much deeper than first imagined. Many today are experiencing debilitating disappointment from mediocre results that began with a burning passion to *win the lost at any cost*. Though you may not be lacking in enthusiasm or zeal, your success may have been sabotaged years ago. You, and/or the people you associate with may be suffering the consequences of being out of step with God.

The scripture states, "All things work together for good to them that love God, to them who are the called according to his purpose." We know we love the Lord. But are we moving in line with His purposes for us? The typical response when we miss the mark is to try and try again. But after a prolonged time of trying, frustration, discouragement and even anger all begin to stalk the trail of the person who keeps trying without seeing results. We have an unseen enemy whose greatest pleasure is to destroy our dreams of having a successful life. Therefore, at a certain juncture, results must be forthcoming. Results are what we believers are promised and what we live for. Jesus said, "Ask, and ye shall receive, that your joy may be full."

FRUSTRATED

"I don't understand it. I've done everything I know to do, and nothing has changed," the preacher cried out in anguish, hoping for some note of sympathy or understanding from the wife of a noted evangelist. Not realizing he had failed to elicit her sympathy but succeeded only in provoking her ire at the statement with the mere implication that all was hopeless. She was an experienced veteran in the ways of God, totally convinced that in times of utter frustration, we were the problem, not God. Coolly and firmly she shot back at him, "That's your problem...you just don't know enough." It was a cold slap, but true. This man was laboring as a result of not having the knowledge he needed to get the job done. He was teetering dangerously on the brink of hopelessness, from simply not knowing enough. God says, "My people are destroyed for the lack of knowledge." It is the classic definition of insanity to keep repeating the same actions while expecting different results. Stop and see if you've missed God.

THE PRICE OF MISSING GOD

The terrible price we pay for missing Him is total abandonment from His protection and His presence. This is not a matter of God forsaking us, but us walking off from Him. Whenever we do, we are on our own. Whether it's an individual who misses God's changes of direction and finds himself suddenly stranded, unable to hear the voice of God, or a once vibrant, growing spirit filled denomination experiencing for the first time an alarming steadily declining membership, the result is the same, panic.

Those of us who have walked with God for any length of time know that what God has approved and ordained will grow. There may be opposition, but the eminent domain of the kingdom of God always wins out. But, if after a time, there is no growth and no progress, something is very wrong. Long before danger, God always informs His people of what's ahead. Then begins the lengthy journey of walking with Him toward the promised goal. From time to time God makes changes and shifts, which are both significant and critical to all who follow Him. To walk with God requires a spirited pace, keeping up with His changes of direction. For that very reason, God has always been adamant against His likeness sculpted into a stationary statue for display. God is constantly moving. When He speaks, He is on the move. Likewise, His words cannot be described as merely ancient literature. His words are alive and powerful, and we must consider His utterance precious.

The power of His words to transform depends upon our cooperation with His every move. Just as fresh as each new morning is, so is the activity of God. Because most of us don't even consider this matter important, we believers are unprepared for an enemy who prides himself on using the latest technological advances to advance his agenda. Too many of us are perfectly satisfied with hearing from God second hand through another man or woman. The unsettling question is, what if they're wrong or out of step with God? Then those who follow them would be blindly following erroneous and/or obsolete information. Jesus warned, "If the blind lead the blind both shall fall into the ditch." No matter how noble their intentions, both will fall into the ditch.

It behooves us to make certain those we follow are walking in step with the move of God, or take precautions that keep us on course should they suddenly digress. It's a tragedy that we have been content to allow so critical a necessity as the quality of our walk with God to rest in the hands of others. For years, some have not even bothered to pick up the Bible to make sure we are in step with His current activities. Sadly, it just doesn't seem that important. But the Lord said, "My people are destroyed for a lack of knowledge."

It is a disturbing fact that God's people have consistently missed His divine shifts. Those times when God, after a period of working His presence and His power in a certain person, mission or movement, abruptly closes shop and moves on. Or similar times, after having given a life-changing revelation, He begins to move into the next phase. He has so much to say to us in so limited time, and we have so very much to learn, but we must fully receive His concepts. They are delivered in segments, line upon line and precept upon precept. The diligent and conscientious person will get into position to catch every word and every phrase. We are advised to live by every word that proceeds out of the mouth of God.

THE TROUBLE WITH PARTIAL REVELATION

I believe that too many religious sects and denominations have been formed around only partial revelation; Bible concepts, only partially understood which needed but lacked further clarity. Clarity that was unfolding just ahead, with a little push of persistence. But the pursuit of more revelation ceased in favor of some other focus. Baptism, tongues, communion, Sabbath days, etc., churches have been established around a limited understanding of every one. Our diverse religious beliefs have, as a result, become at best a patchwork of only pieces of the important whole truths He intended for us to fully embrace.

God has a daunting task of making any significant move in the earth because the very people He intends to bless get left behind. Any divine intervention runs the gamut from cautious acceptance to outright rejection. Our responses to His changes have been as varied as our individual personalities. Some refuse to change and immediately get stuck in the past. Others *freeze frame* to keep things exactly as they are, refusing to change anything. They labor under the misguided notion that to change would displease God. Surprisingly, even those who benefitted from the last miraculous change resist the new change, fearing displacement from their privileged positions. And sadly, some actually have no idea that change ever occurred.

Over the centuries, God has spared no effort to make broad, sweeping changes to benefit mankind. The sacrifice of His son two thousand years ago proves the point. It is a past event that, to this very day, continues to incur the anger and resistance of God's original chosen people, the Jews. Often misunderstood, God continues to change entire dispensations to get us to know more about Him. But whenever He does, His intentions are too often misread and people, His people, continue to lag behind.

Scripture References:

Ephesians 6:10

Isaiah 43:19

Malachi 3:6

Romans 8:28, 37

Hosea 4:6

John 16:24

Matthew 4:4; 15:14

CHAPTER 3
WHEN GOD HAS MOVED ON

In the fall of Adam, we lost everything. Our connection with God was all but totally severed. Contact with Him from that point on was strained and limited. Our familiarity with spiritual principles and revelation immediately began to weaken. At once, the damaging effects of the curse began to permeate the entire universe. And with it, an unrelenting tide of fear and death flooded the whole earth. Fear and death, two forces totally strange to man's existence, not only entered but also ruled the inhabitants of the earth. Unable to resist the forceful current sweeping him away from God, man drifted further and further from his divine home. The swift-moving curse swept him far out into the vast sea of the natural world where God could no longer be seen or detected.

Evicted from Eden, Adam and Eve were banished to a hostile physical world with no chance of returning to the garden. Within the confines of the physical world, only the natural physical things appeared real to man's natural senses. The world of the spirit slowly faded from view and in time totally disappeared. To God, man was "dead," unable to freely communicate with Him. To man, God was now unseen, hidden beyond man's natural sight. Man was yet physically alive, but spiritually, he had lapsed into a comatose state toward God. And without interaction with the life-giving spirit, man was hopeless.

GOD'S PLAN

But God had devised a salvation plan before the world began. That plan included the painstaking resuscitation of man over centuries of time. It would take the calculated entrance of God's Word and the supreme sacrifice of His son, Jesus. First, the Word would be preached to a few individuals, then to a nation, then to thousands and on and on. The plan over the centuries was for fallen man to be completely reconciled with God. Starting with God's firstborn, Jesus, mankind would be resurrected from the dead ultimately to be born again as the children of the Almighty, restored to complete authority in the earth. This divine strategy would unfold in several well-planned stages ending with the full reuniting of God and man in the kingdom of God. The Book of Revelation was written to include the details of the final conquest andcelebration. The plans of God are already set in order and written. The only variable now is man. To honor man's God-given free will, while at the same time keep him on schedule with God's plan for the ultimate success, major adjustments and shifts would be needed. But whatever the change or adjustment, mankind could not afford to be out of step with God.

GOD'S SHIFTS AND CHANGES

Since the fall, God has made numerous shifts and changes in His dealings with us. He is well into the plan He started. But man hasn't been totally cooperative. Our reactions to God's shifts are quite varied. Historically, we can see instances where people stopped everything to camp around a particular move of God. It's similar to traveling by car across certain parts of the country and encountering people who at a certain time in the past did what I call *froze frame* on their culture. Refusing for whatever reason to allow any further changes to their lifestyles, they simply *froze frame*.

All around them, the culture moved with new discoveries, which resulted in new conveniences. But the leadership of their group consciously decided to resist any further conformity. Their handmade wares are sold in the open market as novelties of a bygone age. The people in these societies seem proud to have been able to remain untainted and undisturbed by the undesirable pressures of progress. Some still ride in horse-drawn wagons and live without electricity in their homes. I don't consider this a crime, but it is certainly a more difficult lifestyle than those of us who are enjoying the use of modern technology.

It is a crime, however, when it relates to the people of God, and when it's God who's initiating the change. There is a similar road on which the people of God have traveled which is littered with the campsites of groups who have simply frozen frame on a specific aspect of God. Whether worship days, outward apparel or religious rituals, each has found a comfortable niche and set up camp. Standing ready to resist any attempt to even address the issue by calling it "compromise." Unfortunately, when the barriers were erected to repel change, "fresh revelation" also became a casualty.

God does not have to change. By definition of being God, He already knows all. But man, who is made in the image of God and who by his own doing fell away from God, must be restored to full *God-likeness* (godliness). God has decided in His infinite love that we are well worth the time and expense to get us there. He uses time, effort and resources in a certain strategy to get a desired effect. Then without further explanation, He changes. At times determined by God, major phases of His work with man are completed, and He begins anew. When this happens, those who are not in tune with Him invariably lag behind, working with what God has abandoned.

God never makes a significant change without making His people aware of what He's doing. However, when God selects an individual to inform the people of the coming change, the reaction can be ugly. One who is chosen for this assignment must be ready for the immediate rejection, persecution and in some cases, be prepared to sacrifice his life to get the word to the people. Man in his pride and arrogance far too often stakes his entire life and reputation on one powerful but narrow revelation from God. Therefore, when a servant of the unseen God brings word of a new direction, a violent confrontation ensues. People who fear change are not above using any means at their disposal to rid themselves of those whose words disrupt the status quo. Too many have been killed for bringing word that there's been a change. The martyrs' list of names goes from John the Baptist to Jesus, to Paul and on and on. Each came with a fresh word of change, and each was attacked by those who hated their message. Jesus said, "...that light has come into the world and men loved darkness rather than light."

GOD'S MOVES

Adam and Eve's shocking discovery on the heels of their disobedience was not only their nakedness but also the fact that suddenly everything had changed. They were evicted from Eden and that peaceful time of grace and favor was over. God pronounced the change as they listened without any clue of what was about to happen.

"Cursed is the ground because of you, through painful toil you will eat of it all the days of your life." Having grown accustomed to times of sweet relationship with Adam and Eve in the garden, God Himself would not be untouched by the severe consequences of this curse. He would now be robbed of that joy of fellowship with His new creation for ages to come. From that time on, His dealings with man changed. The innocence of mankind now violated, God drove man out of Eden. This must have seemed so callous to the couple that had moments before enjoyed uninterrupted communion. But it was over, and there was no returning. God had closed the chapter and moved on.

During Noah's generation, God's attention was narrowed to one family who served Him in the midst of a world so wicked; God regretted He had made them. This is the only time it seems that there may have been a question in the mind of God as to whether he could actually go through with the price needed for man's redemption. The wickedness was so great in man that God chose to destroy the entire world. He chose instead to restart creation with Noah's family and a select number of animals. God allowed a hundred years of warning by Noah's message of impending judgment. But once the time allotted was ended, the flood came. The whole earth was covered with water, and whole nations were destroyed.

Noah's generation was reported in the Bible to be

men of renown, mighty men, giants in the earth. Not much more is recorded in the Bible about them, but we can infer that the time in which they lived must have been something to behold. But, no matter how magnificent the times and the people, the decision to change had come and there was no reprieve. God was satisfied to replenish the earth with one family and a shipload of animals. Then again, He moved on.

CHANGE IS CHARACTERISTIC WITH GOD

Change is characteristic with God throughout the Bible. From the time of the first couple's eviction from the garden to Israel's expulsion from the Promised Land, God's plan has always been evolving and changing. Not that He changes his mind in light of the circumstances, but He changes His approach at the end of each phase of His preplanned agenda. Throughout the Bible, we see a pattern. First, a special move of God when people enjoy a special relationship with special works from the Lord. Then an abrupt change when God completes His business and moves on. The problem is, as God moves through His agenda everyone is not in sync with what's happening. It is certainly true that when God makes a change some are moving in step with Him making things happen, some are watching things and others aren't even aware anything at all happened. This is especially true when God performs special acts.

The great daily miracle of manna from Heaven was unlike any other. Bread from Heaven was what it was called. It lasted for years, as long as the children of Israel were wandering in the wilderness. But this great manifestation ceased abruptly when the children crossed the Jordan and became, at once, yesterday's move of God.

Elijah's brook dried up. The private miracle that sustained him during the three-year drought suddenly ended, and Elijah had to move on. With God, how do we stay current and avoid lagging behind? How do we follow His voice and not merely His footprints? How can we know there's a change coming in time enough to prepare for the change and to position our lives in time? Thousands of people are totally oblivious that these changes even occur. In fact, it seems that throughout the Bible whenever God got ready to shift and make a change, He encountered resistance, obstinacy, misunderstanding and apathy. I believe this is where religion has its most disturbing influence.

TRADITIONS, RITUALS AND RELICS

There is a misguided tendency by God's people to enshrine and idolize each of God's moves. Attempting to keep for as long as possible a past move or event. Testimonies abound of the things He used to do. This would be fine if He characteristically made short visits to earth or often departed for trips to far away destinations. The need for "keepsakes" or "relics" then would be obvious. But since He is alive and well and ever present, there should be no need for relics. This ensures that being out of step will continue indefinitely. It is indicative of people who have stopped striving for deeper relationship and further understanding of God but of prideful complacency, satisfied to keep God within understandable limits.

Actually, ancient traditions and rituals began with instructions from God Himself. They were serious instructions meant to teach the people about God and His ways. The second purpose was to give them a foundation for the accumulation of more revelation. Knowledge, especially the volumes we have yet to learn about God, is cumulative. It is best received when delivered in palatable portions. Rituals were meant to be only temporary teaching tools whose purpose was to become symbols that would give way to the real thing. The types and shadows of the Old Testament were to lead us to the image itself, but somewhere we missed it.

Religion with its characteristic fear and lack of understanding held on to the rituals and traditions past the time assigned by God, in effect creating a museum of statues and relics from the past which have no power, except in memory. It was then that Bible characters became powerful only in the pages of the Bible as stories of fantasy and not as real-life experiences. This is indicative of people who have been out of touch with the current move of the living God; who have missed His signals and lost track of His shifts.

Scripture References

Genesis 3:17; 6:4

Joshua 5:12

I Kings 17:7

CHAPTER 4
AN INVITATION TO A REVELATION

What God accomplished and created with His words is yet astounding to our natural minds. In Genesis, the first book of the Bible, we have a vivid picture of Him standing out in the universe creating an entire physical world by speaking words. The scriptures describe the scene like this, "And the earth was without form, and void; and darkness was upon the face of the deep. And the spirit of God moved upon the face of the waters. And God said, "Let there be light: and there was light." In response to the Word of God, an entire dark and void world was changed forever. We understand that even to this very day the universe continues to expand at the speed of light. As observers, we realize that this is the unimpeded power of creation.

He speaks, and the universe responds obediently to whatever He says. There is no opposition to His words. What absolute authority and rule God possesses! This must be the highest level of work and best method of accomplishing a desired goal. It is such a spectacular feat; we are tempted to call it fantasy. This is the creation account taught in churches and Sunday School lessons from my youth to this very day. That God created the earth using words is to every believer an amazing truth. However, as we praise Him for such mighty acts, many are totally unaware of a critically important purpose expressed in creation. That of not just showing His power, but of inviting His children to one of the greatest revelations ever received, of being able to imitate our Father and create through words spoken.

SEPARATION FROM GOD

After the failure of Adam and Eve in the garden, much of our original design was irretrievably lost. Man could never redeem himself by his own ability. It stands to reason that any good father desires his children to grow up and be like him. God is no exception. He sets the highest standard on fatherhood. But we, like the prodigal son, abandoned our good home for the allurements of the enemy. Had it not been for the love of God, there would have been no redemption. When we parted company, God and man walked in totally opposite directions. Although we were made in His image and likeness, we took a road, which continuously descended into death, a complete separation from God. God lamented this separation in saying, "For my thoughts are not your thoughts, neither are your ways my ways, saith the

LORD. For as the heavens are higher than the earth, so are my ways higher than your ways, and my thoughts than your thoughts." A separation of this magnitude was never designed to happen in God's original plan for man. Made in God's image and likeness, man was designed to be a welcomed new arrival into the family of God. His responsibility was to walk in that image, exercising dominion over the entire planet. In this same scripture, God reveals how the head of the family accomplishes His work. He says in essence, "Our ways have parted company, and at this point, they are as distant from each other as Heaven and earth. However, since Heaven ultimately dictates what happens on earth, let Me show you how I do things up here. My Word is like the rain and snow coming from Heaven. Both come from the clouds above and fall to the earth, causing the parched soil and thirsty plants to bring forth and bud. I have the power to send My Word like a messenger carrying out My will upon the earth. It leaves and returns like an unseen spirit moving. But, it cannot return to Me without accomplishing what I sent it to do. Whenever I need something done, I send My Word."

We all expect the mighty God to be able to perform on this level. What we weren't prepared for was God's invitation for us to do the same thing with our words. No one is disturbed or surprised by the fact that God does miracles. It's His nature. What we are surprised about is His apparent expectation that His sons and daughters do likewise. Who would dare think that we *mortals* would be expected to do what God does?

THE INTEGRITY OF THE WORD

God's Word has a well-earned and well-established reputation in this world. Against insurmountable odds, it accomplishes the goal. Through Noah, Abraham, Isaac and Jacob, His Word set its course against the tide of natural laws and physical impossibilities and won. By His Word, a family became the nation of Israel that continues to this day. By His Word, a shepherd boy defeated a giant, became a king and is memorialized in ancient scripture throughout time.

His Word formed the foundation of moral law in the earth by giving us the Ten Commandments. Not ten suggestions to ponder, commandments to obey. His order to Israel was that man, His likeness and image in the earth, was to live by every word that proceeded from His mouth. There was no time to explain the reasons for the commandments, or to explain that there was an unseen enemy preying upon man. Simple obedience to God's Word would shield them from the curse loose in the earth. If they loved and trusted Him, they would follow His instructions to the letter and be blessed. Some obeyed and were blessed beyond their dreams. Others rebelled and met unpleasant consequences.

A DEMONSTRATION OF THE POWER OF WORD

Jesus came on the scene at the right time. *In the fullness of time*, the scriptures say. He had much to say to the world. Not only telling what was on the heart of God but also showing us that we actually have a Father who is God Almighty. The religious sect of that day attempted to kill Him for the very mention of His divine nature. But, He pointed to the miracles that were being performed in their midst as proof of God's divine presence within Him. One day, Jesus conducted a powerful demonstration for His disciples that would forever change their thinking.

He demonstrated the very principle of creation, then taught them how to do the same. In the Book of Mark, Jesus was hungry and saw a fig tree with leaves. And though it was not the season for figs, we understand that if a fig tree had leaves, it usually also had figs. Searching the tree and finding none, Jesus spoke words directly to the tree, cursing it, saying, "No man will ever eat from you again." The next day, the disciples saw the tree lying on its side. They were amazed and brought it to Jesus' attention. Jesus took this time to bring them back to the creation principle of the power of words. He first told them to have faith in God. Or, as the translators tell us, He said, "Have the God kind of faith." He said in essence, if you say to a mountain be removed and don't doubt that what you say is coming to pass, you will have whatever you say, just like your Father. He went on to say (paraphrased), "And when you pray whatever you desire, believe you have received what you prayed for, and you will have it."

Jesus was referring them back to the beginning—the time when God's faith in His words was demonstrated. The Father God spoke words, certain that what He said would come to pass and it did, time and time again. This obviously sounded far-fetched to the disciples. They must have been dumbfounded at the teaching because we have no record of any response whatsoever from any of them. It was a great challenge for them to believe that what they said would come to pass. But, if they expected the same results, they would have to put into action what they learned. Up to that time, it was widely accepted that only God could operate that way. But now, in one brief lesson, Jesus was unveiling the secret to men. Having made plain the mystery of His creative ability; it was obvious that, from that time forth, they would be responsible to act on what they had heard. This was indeed a profound shift that would establish forever within them the knowledge of man's divine ability to create.

IDLE WORDS

What was Jesus saying? In essence, He was saying; God says His words won't return to Him void, or without accomplishing their intended purpose. If the sons of God will follow the same example, and believe that their words won't return empty, they will accomplish in the same manner. The opposite is also true. If, when praying, he doubts that his words will come to pass, he will not be effective.

Jesus now began even to warn them of their "idle" words. Who had ever known or heard such teaching on mere words? That mankind was expected to measure his words and make sure none were spoken without purpose. Jesus warned that every idle word man speaks; he must give an account of at judgment. Idle words are words spoken that have neither faith nor purpose backing them. Idle is defined from the Greek root word "argos" as unemployed, inactive, lazy or useless. Words to God are creative forces. In time, they become reality for the one who believes. With them, God created the universe and with them, the sons of God create their chosen environments.

SPEAK THE WORD ONLY

In His travels, Jesus was also noticeably quite taken with a Roman centurion who caught on to this principle. Apparently, a beloved servant of the officer was sick and near death, and he had come to Jesus to plead for his healing. This man was reportedly a financial supporter of the Jewish people, who had built a synagogue for them. His reverence for the religious laws of the Jews was apparent when he stated that he felt unworthy for Jesus, the Son of God, to come into his home. (He cited the law that forbade Jews from socializing in the homes of Gentiles).

To Jesus' astonishment, the centurion demonstrated more faith than any Jew he had encountered. He had clearly understood the entire principle by observing Jesus and comparing it to his own experience as a commander in the Roman army. He said, "I make a command and my servants respond. You command and sickness and demons respond. Speak a word only and my servant will be healed." Jesus was astonished and called it great faith. He said, "I haven't found this kind of faith, not in all of Israel." Here before Him was a man, a Gentile, who would believe the power of words spoken.

The revelation of this principle was indeed a major shift in the way God deals with His people. The church world is yet grappling with its truth. Some to this day have chosen to ignore it. But we know that Jesus only spoke what He heard His Father say. It must be God's will that our words create as His did in the beginning. Jesus opened it to all who dare to believe. He said, "**Whosoever** shall say to the mountain, 'Be thou removed and be thou cast into the sea,' and shall not doubt in his heart but shall believe the things he saith shall come to pass he shall have **whatsoever** he saith." If we allow ourselves to miss this principle, whether it's because of opposition, offense or traditional mindsets, we will lose out. This is an invitation to participate in the exciting work of creating with words. A privilege extended to all believers by the grace of God.

Scripture References:

Genesis 1:2

Deuteronomy 8:3

Isaiah 55:8

John 14:24

Luke 7:2-10

Mark 11:12-14, 23

Matthew 12:36, 8:5-10

CHAPTER 5
TWO REVELATIONS THAT CHANGED EVERYTHING

To everyone who has secretly or openly questioned God about the predicaments into which they were born, there may be some consolation. Birth defects, inherited childhood diseases, child neglect and abuse have always evoked more questions than answers. We often wonder why innocent children are afflicted with such unfair circumstances. Some of us, for whatever the reason, from the day we were born, have had to suffer so much more than others. It causes us to resign ourselves to the mantra that although life isn't fair, God is still good.

Through the depths of affliction and deprivation in our childhood experiences, some of the greatest revelations ever known to man have come. Insights have come to light that have forever changed our old thinking to a fresh walk and relationship with the Lord. No credit whatsoever is given to the adversity itself, however.

Horrendous circumstances and cruel treatment are not the work of our Father, but rather the handiwork of a hateful adversary. Make no mistake, Satan's agenda is always to kill, steal and destroy. But, glory and praises go to the Lord who delivers us from every affliction.

In 1934, a child was born barely alive. From the tell-tale blue hue of his skin to the faintness of his breath, he had little chance of living. Afflicted with a deformed heart and an incurable blood disease, he had little chance of survival. Because of internal complications, he was abnormally small and could not breathe properly. The young child was barely clinging to life when his grandmother snatched him and began to work to save his life.

Because of his poorly developed internal organs, it was diagnosed that he would not live to see adulthood. As a child, he could never play like other children. If he ran any distance, he would immediately lose consciousness and collapse. Instead of growing stronger as time progressed, he grew weaker. As expected, the other kids did not spare him any pain. They never missed an opportunity to point out his weaknesses for open ridicule. He was teased, taunted and left out of the normal play activities so many take for granted. As he reached his teens, the disease became full-blown and started completely shutting down his body. This was the precursor to what was promised to be imminent death.

Kenneth Hagin was that child born with physical conditions that were considered at thattime to be fatal. With a deformed heart and an incurable blood disease, he was sure to die at an early age. At age fifteen, he became totally bedfast with only one thing certain. His short life was soon ending. Ending, that is, if it weren't for the intervention of a miracle. Hagin didn't die. He lived well into his eighties. He somehow found the key to believing God for the impossible.

Nothing came easy. He often spoke of the utter hopelessness he felt, and of the frustration of reading God's promises of healing and of his inexplicable failure to receive. He also spoke of how he prayed hour after hour, day after day begging and pleading to be healed, to no avail. He spoke of the times his heart actually stopped beating. Feeling himself slipping helplessly into death, he fought the inevitable with all that he could muster. He said that the headboard of his bed was filled with scratches where he tried to cling to it to stay alive. Though his struggle seemed hopeless in the face of advancing paralysis, he received a revelation from the Lord that saved his life and revolutionized the entire Christian world.

> *"Therefore I say unto you, What things soever ye desire, when ye pray, believe that ye receive them, and ye shall have them."—Mark 11:24*

As he read this scripture, he stood on its words before God and proclaimed, "I do believe. If you say I don't believe Lord, you'd be lying. I do believe." He was adamant about the fact that he did believe but was yet desperate for the key that would make it work for him. What the Lord said to him next changed everything. The Lord said, "You believe alright, as far as you know. But the rest of the scripture goes with the first part of the verse. "...believe ye receive them and ye shall have them."

Hagin acknowledged that of everything he had done, he hadn't believed that part. The light came on. He was to believe he received while he yet felt no change in his body. The revelation was that while you are yet seeing and feeling the opposite in your body, the miracle is actually yours. It's at the point you believe that you receive it. It could not work as long as he waited until he physically felt a change. He was to secure the miracle by believing he received in spite of, and in the face of symptoms that were contrary. He took hold of this revelation and stopped for a few moments to believe the Word and to thank God for his healing. Then the Lord told him that people who are well need to be up out of bed. He said, "That's right; I'm going to get up." Then he pulled his six foot one inch, ninety-pound frame to the side of his bed, swung his paralyzed legs over the side, and began to stand. After a last-ditch effort from the enemy to frighten him out of taking a faith step, he stood upright. Miraculously, the power of God kicked in. From that moment on, he was healed. In the ensuing days, as he continued to stand tenaciously on those words against the enemy's counterattack, he kept his focus and prevailed, and was never bedfast again.

Believe that ye receive and ye shall have became the words that changed everything. It was as if God was waiting for believers to get the revelation. Who would have thought that such a phrase would have such an impact on the entire Body of Christ? The ministry of Kenneth Hagin grew and prospered around this powerful phrase. This revelation was spread throughout the world.

Have you changed with this revelation? Is this included as part of your prayer when you pray? When we pray we must *believe that we receive*, then we shall have. This changes the nature and focus of all prayers and takes us all into a new dimension. It takes the responsibility off of God and places it squarely on us. Now, we know prayers will only be effective if the people praying believe they receive when they're praying. Anything less will be ineffective. In all our dealings with God, we must *believe we receive*. This is real faith in God. This is also using the God kind of faith. To believe we receive when we cannot see or feel a thing takes us to a new level.

All the struggles Hagin endured with that illness abruptly ended when he simply believed that he received and acted upon it. God was now released to perform among believers a new cadre of blessings, which would know no limits. No longer could we be held in bondage to our natural senses or our limited experiences when it came to faith. We learned that when we *believe we receive*, we take the devil to unfamiliar ground. He is then soundly defeated by our faith.

PART II

The second revelation that totally jarred our limited thinking out of its coma occurred as Hagin was receiving a vision from the Lord. He said that in the vision, God promised to teach him about the devil, demons and demon possession and suddenly an impish figure appeared in the very vision where Jesus was talking. The demon spread something like a smoke screen or dark cloud obscuring his view of Jesus. It then started jumping up and down between them making a shrill sound, drowning out the voice of Jesus with the words: "Yakety Yak, Yakety Yak, Yakety Yak!" According to Hagin, this went on for some time. He thought to himself, "Why doesn't Jesus do something about that? Doesn't he know I can't hear what He's saying?" Finally after some time had elapsed, annoyed by the very audacity of this interruption, Hagin took it upon himself to command the spirit in the name of Jesus to shut up and get out. At his command, the spirit immediately stopped. Then the cloud disappeared, and the demon scurried off like a whipped puppy. Hagin recounted that Jesus then said something that absolutely flew into the face of all the traditional thinking of our time. Jesus said to him, "If you hadn't done something about that I couldn't have." Knowing that he couldn't be hearing what he thought he just heard, Hagin, like the rest of us who believe there's nothing Jesus can't do, challenged the statement. "Lord," he said, "You mean you wouldn't, not you couldn't." "No," Jesus said, "I said I couldn't." After a few repetitions of this unsettling disclosure, Jesus explained what He meant.

He explained that nowhere in the New Testament scriptures does it state that He or the Father will do anything about the devil. It's written that you will cast out devils. You will resist the devil, and he'll flee from you. You are to give no place to the devil. That's because when Jesus rose from the grave and said, "All power in Heaven and in earth is given unto me." He immediately transferred His power to man. Jesus said to His disciples "...you go now I'll be with you." Since He transferred the power to man, we must now do something about the devil or nothing will be done. In the vision, Jesus said to Hagin, "I immediately delegated My authority on earth to the Church, and now I can work only through the Church, for I am the Head of the Church."

From further study of the subject, a great revelation blossomed. It was the life-changing revelation of the authority we have as believers. The first two chapters in the Book of Ephesians describe an exceeding great power that has been released in and for man. Man is now described as quickened together with Christ and raised up and seated together in heavenly places in Christ. No longer is Jesus alone doing the works of God. Now Jesus has taken the position as head of a large body of believers working in sync as the Body of Christ.

The authority He has we now have. Since we know Jesus is seated at the right hand of God, that makes this revelation even more astounding. Mankind has actually been elevated into a position of high authority, seated at the right hand of God with Jesus. Again, this is a revelation. We cannot fully grasp it with our natural minds. We must take time to meditate on it, asking the Lord to illuminate our minds. This is a revelation that has changed everything! The scriptures bear this out in Romans. It is stated in chapter five that we who receive the gift of righteousness and the abundance of God's grace (undeserved favor) shall reign in this life through Jesus Christ our Lord. We are to reign in this life. Even now, we are in authority.

In 2003, Kenneth Hagin passed away but not before these two rich revelations had illuminated almost the entire Christian world. Yet we should not forget that all of it came from a desperate beginning with the birth of a child, born just barely alive. A child whose first years were characterized by weakness, sickness, struggle and the serious prospect of an early death. It is amazing how

God can reverse every intended curse into a blessing. He turned the violently inflicted stripes of Jesus into streams of healing, and He turns our deepest anguish and suffering into a greater revelation of His love. He will also miraculously transform the hardships you have endured into blessings for many.

Scripture References:

Ephesians 1:19; 2:1,6; 4:47   James 4:7

John 10:10   Mark 11:24; 16:16

Matthew 28:18-20

CHAPTER 6
WHAT HAPPENED TO MY JOY

Few experiences in the life of believers can be compared to what God works in us through the feeling of joy. He uses the ebb and flow of this awesome feeling to teach us some lasting principles. Through releasing it and withdrawing it, we are made to learn the importance of joy even as a temporary good feeling. However, it is meant to be much more. We learn in dry seasons that it must be more abundant and much deeper than the way it originally arrives.

The first days of our deliverance from sin are heavenly. The whole world is wonderful to us. The sunshine is brighter, and the love of God is permeating our entire existence. We don't want to hurt a soul, and our commitment to the Lord is strong. We can feel the joy of the Lord as a tangible presence, and we feel pity for those who lack such an experience. The one question we have is, why did we wait so long to make Jesus the Lord of our lives? Life is grand and glorious. Can we expect the feeling of joy to last? Not for long. At least not in its present form. The joy of the Lord has an eternal purpose that the Lord begins to reveal as time progresses.

Many newly saved Christians have been filled with the joyful feeling of salvation, making life more than they could have imagined. Because of its constant flow in the beginning, they assume it to be the permanent presence of the Lord. And in a sense, they are correct, but only partially so. It is the presence of the Lord, but there is much more. They assume this is God's calling card because, at first, His presence always comes with a feeling of joy. Such joy that it appears to have ignited a fire on the inside. Motivated by the fire and the feeling, no task is too great or distance too far to accomplish for God.

During this time, they sense a nearness to God so much so they feel as if they could actually touch Him. The constant flow changes their behavior to that which seeks to be in solitude more often in order to experience the feeling of joy again and again. They begin to shun the company of people for fear of weakening their relationship with God. It's what I call the *honeymoon phase*, a time when all is well, and God answers every beck and call. Some have even looked down on more mature believers who may not be experiencing such ecstasy in their lives right now. Judging ordinary believers as if they are of a lesser walk with God, these newcomers feel an inward superiority of experience with the Lord. They sense themselves floating in the clouds far above ordinary Christians plodding on the earth below. However, having allowed them ample time to enjoy this sublime experience for a few months, God characteristically shifts and, without warning, the joy suddenly vanishes.

For the first time in their walk with God, to awaken without the feeling of joy is a sobering jolt. Some immediately assume because their joy is gone they have sinned or displeased the Lord in some way. Satan quickly joins in to accuse them, making matters worse. Others wither from the sudden loss, eventually falling backward into their former lifestyle, unwilling to proceed without the feeling. The struggle is on as each tries to free themselves from this dry and thirsty land. Without the feeling of joy, the new believer feels himself abandoned by God and wonders, "Where has the Lord gone?"

The gifts of God are so wonderful; we all have a tendency to abuse them. Gifts are so great; we want to use them for our own pleasure and comfort without regard for their intended purpose. Let's examine for a moment God's purposes for extending to the newly saved believer the feelings of joy:

1. **God uses joy to draw mankind close to him.** The scriptures state, "in the presence of the Lord is the fullness of joy and at his right hand are pleasures evermore..."

2. **God will withdraw the feeling of joy from our lives when it's for us to learn how to trust Him when we can't trace Him.** This is much more than a surface relationship with the Lord. It's an abiding trust in what we've learned about the faithfulness of the Lord.

3. **God is also training us to make a decision by the exercise of our will instead of feelings.** It is much more mature a relationship when we serve God in spite of what we feel.

4. **God is teaching us that praises can be given as a simple response either to a feeling of joy or, much more importantly, to create joy in absolutely dreadful circumstances.** The example of Paul and Silas comes to mind. When after being publicly beaten and thrown in jail, the two missionaries openly pray and sing praises to God. The great earthquake that occurred freed them from their chains, opened the prison and caused the jailor and his family to be saved. The sacrifice of praise is welcomed by the Lord as a fitting sacrifice.

5. **Withdrawing the feeling of joy can help the beginner learn God is present and His Word true whether you feel Him or not.** No one can say it is not pleasant to feel the joy. But God must at times withdraw the joyful feel-

ings to mature us in this way. The higher level of living designed for the believer is one that must be able to weather the tests of feelings that result from exposure to all forms of adversity. Well aware of the trickery of the enemy, withdrawing and releasing feelings of joy helps us to place our joy deeply into our inner man. As a result, we base it upon a more eternal foundation that cannot be moved, which is the Word of God.

What the young believer may not know is that within a relatively short period after a dry season, the feeling of joy returns for his or her enjoyment. It will return for a season and then depart again for a season. But God is teaching a valuable lesson here. Nothing is to be held as permanent except His Word. Everything has a time and a season. Joy, no matter how wonderful, is not to be confused with His total self. God is joy and much more.

JOY AS A HINDRANCE

Entire denominations have built their programs on the feeling of joy. I have participated in and spoken in churches and meetings where services keep it as their central focus. Joy is a wonderful aspect of living for God, but when it is the single most important aspect of an entire evening, revelation suffers. Weighty principles are cast aside in this setting in favor of more palatable promises. As a result, preachers, in order to make certain they'll be invited again, will discard serious messages for more shallow fare. Because even with a serious lack of substance and revelation, ministers can, without spending time with God, raise the roof by stirring up joyful feelings. A charismatic delivery and a decent singing voice can usually carry the moment.

Speaking on lighthearted subjects that make people forget their struggles will also move the crowd quickly under control, then the forceful repetition of key phrases and clichés is also enough to bring the people to their feet. This skill does not require purity of lifestyle nor submission to the Holy Spirit. It is the talent displayed by entertainers before any audience. In such meetings, the atmosphere is charged like a huge pep rally with shouting, swirling and dancing. Each presenter is expected to add to the pitch and the fervor by stoking the flame with more and more emotion. The meetings have lots of excitement as the people are caught up in the celebration, but when the party atmosphere is over very little substantive enlightenment is gained.

The speaker and the attendees are physically worn out afterward with very little Word to grow by. There were numerous times after preaching, leaving the audience reeling with joy, that I changed my sweat-soaked clothing with remorse, knowing that I had missed an opportunity toenlighten, and instead succumbed to the pressure to feed them more joy. Everything in God has balance. Like the child who must be restricted from too much sweet stuff, the children of God must be fed a balanced diet. Otherwise, they form an unhealthy addiction to hype, returning again and again to get an emotional fix. I wholeheartedly believe that the joy of the Lord is important and that service time should be a time of celebration, except when it's done at the expense of revelation.

Except people receive fresh revelation from the Lord, they cannot grow, and they will miss God's best. Missing God is tragic to our generation. There is no substitute. God moves on whether we chose to give attention to Him or not. I consider this unfortunate for any group. Many serious aspects of the spirit cannot be delivered in such an atmosphere. Services dominated by hype in time become predictable displays. Many, as a result, remain immature in important areas of the spirit, never having sat still long enough to receive deeper revelation.

TARRYING FOR THE HOLY GHOST

My denomination believed in *tarrying* for the Holy Ghost. This was a teaching handed down from the elders as a proven method for being filled with the spirit. The word *tarry* means to wait. And we designed tarrying service to wait on the infilling of the Holy Spirit. At the young age of 16, I desperately wanted to receive the

Holy Ghost. Partly because of the unspeakable joy that those who received Him said they experienced. I decided that no matter what it took, I was going to receive. Little did I know what it took.

We were all directed into a small room where the seekers were to be essentially guided into this heavenly experience. We were instructed to stand or kneel and focus on Jesus. Then we were to repeat the praise *Hallelujah* or the name, *Jesus*, over and over. The tarry room workers would come alongside and say, "Let go" or "Hold on" or "That's it, let the Lord have His way." You were discouraged from taking a rest, or touching your face, or scratching or wiping your mouth. To do so was a sure sign to the altar workers that you were still thinking about yourself and hadn't focused on the Lord.

You were just supposed to call on Jesus. Whoever called on Jesus, we believed would be *saved*, which to us meant spirit filled. If there was any more labor-intensive exercise in church than tarrying, I didn't know it. At each service, I dreaded what I would have to endure, but I was desperate. This involved hours and hours of kneeling, sweating and calling on Jesus. It was ugly and earthy, musty and sweaty, in some cases like actual childbirth, but somehow people received the Holy Spirit. I heard scores of people after hours of tarrying speak with tongues. It disturbed me that we had to work so hard for something that was supposed to be a free gift.

I was told that when the Holy Ghost came, unspeakable joy would fill my being. I was anticipating a heavenly experience. That's not what happened to me. I tarried for days and weeks. I didn't know why I hadn't received. I could not understand why it was so difficult to reach God. I prayed, repented, cried and begged without any response. Each tarrying service that ended without me receiving the Holy Spirit was so disappointing. In those days, we knew very little about believing; we were acting upon the little we knew. Because of that, I believe God blessed in spite of us, not because of us. Finally, after about approximately a year of tarrying, when I wasn't thinking about receiving, I did. As I knelt tarrying, I heard someone speaking in tongues. The voice was coming from inside me. Surprisingly enough, it was me. The words exploded from my insides like the boom from a cannon. Thank God, I was filled.

But one thing I didn't discuss with anyone was the fact that I didn't experience the joy they talked about. I felt power deep inside my inner man. I spoke in tongues, but I didn't feel the joy unspeakable that they had reported. My lesson was learned early about believing with the feeling of joy. I had none in the beginning. My walk with God was subsequently from a different perspective. I was filled without the feeling. My denomination encouraged and expected the outward display of inner joy. There had to be an outward sign.

When we came together, the room rocked with our leaping, dancing and shouting. Months later as I prayed seeking it, the long-anticipated joy began to pour in. It was tangible and wonderful, truly joy unspeakable. It filled my being. But by that time I had matured. To this day, I cannot explain the reason my experience was different, but I know I was filled with His presence and power. I've long since learned how to believe God without having to work so hard, and I have taught it to others.

GOD WILL ALWAYS DO A NEW THING

When we walk with God, we have to be ready for change. We have to be ready for His shifts when He completes a project and totally departs from everything associated with it. This can be a very serious matter indeed and quite disturbing to God's people. What if it's everything you've built your life around over the past years? What if it involves leaving the people you've grown to love and admire? What if you've built your ministry or your business around the very thing God has departed from? One would think that when dealing with the God who never changes, things would remain constant. But to our surprise, God shifts, and we must adapt to stay in His current move.

At seventy-five years old, Abraham was instructed by God to leave his home and his family to go into a place that he would show him. Who can imagine leaving home and family to travel to an undisclosed location at that age? But because he obeyed, he was greatly blessed. After years of waiting for the miracle of his son Isaac, Abraham was told by God to offer him as a sacrifice. In effect ending at once a wonderful time in the lives of Abraham and Sarah. They had believed and received their miracle and were enjoying this work of God. But Abraham faithfully made the change and began to carry out the fresh word from God. Off he went with his miracle son to offer him up. At the very last moment, before Isaac would have been killed, God changed. We don't want to think of what would have transpired had not Abraham remained open to God's shift.

I didn't know as a young minister that God would do such a thing in our time, not to the degree I would learn it as I grew in the ministry. For years, I labored under the concept that God never changes. Malachi states, "I am the Lord, I change not." To me, that meant that our understanding of what He stated or did was always to be protected and revered as eternal truth. Whatever the standard was regarding lifestyle, dress codes, habits, etc., nothing was to change. It was to be preached and protected against any tampering. After all, our leaders from the Lord had received these standards, and everyone knew that people change, but not God.

However, it became evident through the years that so often we receive God's Word with limited understanding, thinking we really understand what He said. Only to find out at a future date with a little more revelation, we really didn't have a clue. We may indeed have heard and correctly recorded what was said, but what He meant by what He said is revealed as more *light* comes. As the light of revelation comes, we begin to really comprehend what God meant. Then, though it may be embarrassing and humiliating because of the stance we took, change is required. Change comes hard in church. Beliefs, even if found to be in error, die long lingering deaths, taking with them far too many casualties.

The truth of the matter is that God Himself doesn't change in character or power. However, He has reserved the right to do a *new thing*. God prefaces this statement with the words, "Remember ye not the former things, neither consider the things of old." It is evident that He reserves the right to change things to the point that He doesn't want us even to remember what was before. I am amazed that something as sacred as the Law of Moses would ever become obsolete. It was given by the very voice of God Himself. Having been received directly from God with violent thundering and earthquakes, surely, this law would never have an end! But it ended. Even more startling is the fact that the end was orchestrated by God.

Centuries of history, laws, rituals, habits and routines were all brought to a close with the coming of Jesus. Laws that were the subjects of lifetimes of study for the priests, scribes and Pharisees, that also generated business for shepherds and farmers as thousands of livestock, were required for the daily sacrifices. These were laws that gave the priests their privileged status and the Pharisees and scribes significant sources of income and wealth. Around which the entire Jewish culture had its existence. Jesus notified them that the time set for the law had been completed and new preaching of something called the kingdom of God was now replacing the old. Looking at it in this light, one can imagine the collective shock at the audacity of this carpenter's son to even suggest such a thing. A sizeable portion of the economy would be disrupted. But he was not merely suggesting His words were the very declaration of the coming of a new covenant.

In the Gospels, Jesus was persecuted for actions they thought were contrary to the law and ultimately crucified. His crucifixion was celebrated by those who hated the changes brought about with His liberation and blessing of the multitudes. The gospel of Jesus Christ was summarily dismissed by the established religion as a new heresy. They were unaware that this was God Himself changing the entire spiritual landscape. The fact that religion was also the law of the land made it a life-threatening act to even suggest change. Some religious offenses and sinful acts could result in death.

Years after the resurrection, Paul made the statement that the same law, which was so sacred to the Jews, was just a temporary measure instituted by God until living by faith came. Both Jesus and Paul were persecuted by shocked and angry people who were ready to kill them for the message of change they brought. But change came, and the law in one fail stroke became passé. Sadly, there are numbers of people who are still living by the law today, but its time has passed.

KNOWLEDGE IS EVER CHANGING

Knowledge is always only in part. Knowledge is also cumulative. First, we learn the basics, and then move on to more complicated concepts. We begin to realize that God has planned for us to learn things that are far beyond our present level of understanding. God himself uses this teaching pattern. He started out with the children of Israel, teaching them that they were His chosen people. They enjoyed preferences few nations can boast of. Understandably, they made much of the fact that they were Abraham's descendants as well as the fact that they introduced the world at large to the only true God. But this privileged position did not absolve them of the responsibility of staying current with the move of God. When the Lord began to reach out to heathen nations, there was shock and resistance. To include these uncircumcised nations in the blessings that they alone enjoyed was unthinkable. However, as time progressed, they found that the Lord actually had a plan all along to save the heathens who were considered by them to be no higher than dogs.

God planned from the beginning that we were destined to be sons of God. His task was to get that message across to His people who were not only slaves to Pharaoh but unbeknownst to them, slaves to the Satan as well. Satan has very little mention in the Old Testament. One can infer from the silence about the devil that there was not much known about him. As a consequence, both good and evil would be perceived as coming from God. Job said, "the Lord giveth and the Lord taketh away; blessed be the name of the Lord." To the casual observer this was an accurate statement, but under closer scrutiny, a more accurate assessment would be: Job prospered greatly under the care of God. It was only when he was touched by the hand of Satan that he began to suffer disease, loss and death. So, a more accurate statement would be, "the Lord giveth, and the devil kills, steals and destroys."

What dissonance that must have caused in their minds to love a God thought to be responsible for both healing and making sick. They feared to say His name casually for fear of saying it in vain and incurring His wrath. His presence made them tremble. None but the most holy would dare approach and even then with great fear. It wasn't until Jesus came that He clarified this misconception. He said, "the thief comes not but for to steal and to kill and to destroy, but I am come that they might have life and have it more abundantly." He also said, "Every city or house divided against itself shall not stand" implying that God is not working both ends of the spectrum by making sick and making well, or blessing and destroying. This underscored the difference between the agenda of the devil and that of God.

GREAT CHANGES

Abraham

Abraham could not have been expected to grasp the full impact of the reason God forced him to endure the range of emotions evoked by the command to sacrifice his only son—a son he had believed for and waited twenty-five years to receive. This was used to test the commitment of Abraham to God and ultimately for God to swear an oath to Abraham of greater blessings. But He was also speaking to the ages to come. God was revealing to him and all who would read his story the depth of His own feelings as a father sacrificing his only begotten son. This was required to save mankind centuries later. Abraham was spared at the last moment. God as a Father, who had also waited centuries for His only begotten Son, was not.

Moses

The great and powerful ministry of Moses, which included the parting of the Red Sea, The Ten Commandments written by the hand of God, the Manna and the Holy Tabernacle still leaves our minds reeling at the glory of that dispensation. The Bible describes the glory of that time as so great the Israelites could not look upon Moses' face because of its brilliance. It declares it to be the **ministry of condemnation**, which was to pass away. God took the lives and experiences of a whole generation of people and made them mere symbols of future happenings. Their laws and traditions, though rich in experiences with God and His Word, were nonetheless just *types and shadows* or symbols of what was to be revealed. To them, it was a very real-life experience they witnessed, to Him temporary measures in preparation for things to come.

Jesus

The long-awaited Messiah Himself, Jesus operated in a ministry, which far exceeded all of His predecessors. The Gospels Matthew, Mark, Luke and John describe in great detail His birth and His great ministry. The whole world continues to be affected by Him today. As we read the scriptures about His miraculous ministry, it shows that time after time, He saved the day with His mighty power. He turned the religious world of that time upside down. His followers at that time were so blessed by His very presence; they could not conceive of Him departing. His power was so great He even exercised it over the ancient enemy, death, and brought Lazarus and others back to life.

He showed the love and ability of God like no other. The problem with reading the accounts of Jesus is that we are subtly rocked to sleep, accepting the notion that all the power was received by and continues to rest with Him. Further study shows that His authority and power was transferred to His followers. We continue to expect that, as in the Gospels, if we can summon Jesus, He will take care of the problem today. This, unfortunately, is missing the point. Jesus said, "...in that day ye shall ask me nothing, Verily, verily, I say unto you, Whatsoever ye shall ask the Father in my name, he will give it you." He also stated, "Verily, verily, I say unto you, He that believeth on me, the works that I do shall he do also: and greater works than these shall he do: because I go unto my Father." We may not have caught the message given here. Jesus came not only to do the great works, but also to show us how to do them so we could begin to operate in our legitimate authority. He was not the Savior only, but also the example of how to live as a spirit filled believer in our authority. The power He possessed is ours to live by.

Too many people are still praying to bring Jesus to

continue to do the work needed. But Jesus lived to show us how, so we could begin to operate in the authority that is ours. We continue to revere His works, missing the point of His coming, which was to redeem us and to restore all which was lost in the fall of Adam. Healing diseases, raising the dead and defeating spiritual forces was nothing new for God, but it was nothing short of miraculous to fallen man. The greatest miracle was that now all of mankind who believed would be able to do these feats.

Upon the death, burial and resurrection of Jesus, God shifted and began a new move. For centuries, few individuals perceived that everything had changed. Many thought that Jesus' statement; "all power is given unto me in heaven and in earth," meant that everything was still in Heaven in the hands of Jesus. Few realized that Jesus had transferred the authority on earth to the Church, which he now called His own body.

Paul

Years after the resurrection of Jesus, His disciples took up the mantle and preached theGospel everywhere they went. One, in particular, Paul, left on record many of the great things that were done in the name of Jesus. His untiring labor to establish churches throughout the then known world is nothing short of astounding. He left a lucrative position in the established Jewish religion to bring the gospel to the Jews and the barbarians. His writings form the majority of the entire New Testament. His insights and revelations written are the basic beliefs upon which the entire Christian faith now stands.

His ministry was so powerful both in word and demonstration of the power of God that many revere him as the final word in everything. His life and sacrifice set a standard that few to this very day can reach. But even his life was not the end, according to the Word of God. His work is not the epitome, as some would think. We really believe that no one we know can do the things that Paul did. He is viewed as attaining the highest. But even Paul regarded it not as the ceiling, but the foundation. With all due respect, and much is due to the awesome works done by him, his work was only to be the foundation upon which the next installment of the work of God is to be built.

The Gifts

By Paul's writings, we learned that certain people in the Body of Christ are gifts sent for a specific purpose. Some call them the five-fold ministry as mentioned in the Book of Ephesians chapter four. The purpose of these gifts is "for the perfecting of the saints, for the work of the ministry, for the edifying of the body of Christ." Church in this day has been greatly impacted by these ministry gifts, namely apostles, prophets, evangelists, pastors and teachers. Some churches have accepted these gifts; others have resisted and limited their experiences to the pastoral gift. Whatever the response, God is moving in these gifts in this time.

In order to be fully supplied, we must recognize their existence and work together to be affected by each of them. Those who resist, find their churches missing key elements of the maturation of their members. Pastors seem to be the more plentiful in number and have the greater influence in the lives of the members. But some church leaders, because of bad experiences in the past, will not allow these gifts to function in their churches. As a pastor, I cringed on many occasions at the things said and done in the name of "gifts" in special services. I had to clean up many messes made by self-centered ministers who had no idea of the lasting damage they were doing by their words and actions. "Fruits, flakes and nuts" seemed to surface whenever leniency was given for the "Spirit to have His way." In spite of the craziness, these gifts were ordained by God for a godly purpose.

When operating properly, they are of inestimable value to believers. Not only in the services they conduct, but also in aiding each believer in finding their life assignments. However, once again as powerful and wonderful these may be, they have, according to the Word of God, a definite end time. The Book of Ephesians states,

"Till we all come in the unity of the faith, and of the knowledge of the Son of God, unto a perfect man, unto the measure of the stature of the fulness of Christ..." The word *till* means until the time when this happens. When this is achieved, these gifts will have fulfilled their usefulness and purpose, and there will be need for a shift or a change.

We who operate in the gifts are supposed to work ourselves out of a job accomplishing our purpose. That's a bit frightening for some because they question, "What will I do if I'm not needed to pastor or prophesy?" Because of this fear, some leaders have clamped down on all movement within their ministries hoping to stop any change that might affect their position. I know this is usually based on a fear of loss of income and/or influence, which for some is a legitimate concern. But how exciting it will be to find out what the next move of God is once we actually complete our ministry assignments. The anointing for these gifts has been so awesome in many cases, what could be next?

I have heard denominational people say in a prideful manner, "We have the truth here!" As if to say, "we have a monopoly on the truth." Yet we all know that there is so much yet to learn about God. How can such a claim be made seriously? The more we learn, the more we realize we must continue to learn. The daunting task undertaken by God is that He must use present day established truths as a foundation to take us further. We must cooperate by remaining pliable for the inevitable adjustments to our thinking. I believe we are in for more and more revelation in the coming months.

Scripture References:

Acts 16:25	Ephesians 2:20; 3:19; 4:13
Galatians 3:23-24	Isaiah 43:19
Malachi 3:6	Matthew 12:15
Psalm 16:11	Romans 10:6, 7
I Corinthians 13:12	II Corinthians 3:9
Luke 16:16; 24:49	John 10:10; 14:12; 16:16, 23

CHAPTER 7
PETER'S PREJUDICE

We incorrectly assume that the apostles were always in perfect harmony with God. Some might say, "After all, didn't they write the Bible? Didn't they walk with Jesus?" Yes, they did, but that did not instantaneously deliver them from their prejudices—even after receiving the indwelling Holy Spirit. Peter was one such individual who walked with Jesus. He also operated in such an awesome demonstration of the power that even his shadow contained healing for the sick. Yet after all of that, he yet succumbed to the sway of the Jewish laws from which God had already departed. Now a well-respected leader among Jewish Christians, Peter apparently was not ready to completely leave what God had long abandoned. Although he was entrusted by Jesus with the "keys to the kingdom," his neglect to follow completely God's change hindered the transition.

Peter was comfortable as long as the law of circumcision was still observed (although incorrectly) as part of the qualifications for receiving salvation; for Jesus was a circumcised Jew as well as His disciples. Living among the Jews, circumcision was the only option. It appeared to them that this was the reason God could operate so effectively among them. Their deliberate exclusion of Gentiles was further fueled by the fact that Jesus gave the disciples power over unclean spirits, commanding them not to go among the Gentiles or the Samaritans, but to keep the preaching of the gospel and the power exclusively for the "lost sheep of the house of Israel."

After Jesus' resurrection, Peter seemed comfortable to continue keeping vestiges of Jewish law along with his newfound salvation. He yet followed the strict Jewish practice of separation from the Gentiles, not keeping company with and, unless spoken to first, not even speaking to them. But in spite of this, Peter was the very one God chose to reveal His next drastic change to. Apparently, in Acts chapter ten, Peter was by the seaside lodging with a man named Simon, a tanner by trade who lived in the seaside village called Joppa. The scripture states that Peter was hungry and went up to the roof of the house while he waited for the meal to be prepared.

In a vision, God lowers a sheet before Peter filled with divers types of wild animals, creeping things and birds. Peter is told to rise, kill and eat. Appalled by the mere suggestion that he eat something considered by the Jewish law to be unclean, Peter balks at this command saying, "I have never eaten anything that is common or unclean." Then God does something quite unexpected. He states, "What I have cleansed don't you call common or unclean." Quite disturbed by the unsavory prospect of eating animal flesh he considered unclean, Peter again refuses. But God repeats the process of lowering the sheet twice more to emphasize His point. At the end of the vision, Peter is warned again with the same words, "What God has cleansed, do not call common or unclean." Peter awakes out of the vision perplexed at what this meant. Then the Holy Spirit immediately informs him that some men are coming looking for them. He is to go with these men without hesitation or prejudice in the fact that they are Gentiles.

This visit was not without risk. Only the Holy Spirit himself could direct him to do this. Doing it would certainly violate the Jewish law against having any fellowship with non-Jews, and there were sure to be repercussions. Gentiles were uncircumcised and therefore to the Jews, unclean. Unknown to Peter at that time was the fact that he was about to use the "keys to the kingdom" mentioned by Jesus to open the kingdom of God to nations of these so-called unclean people and ultimately to the entire world. God was changing everything—tearing down old boundaries and opening up glorious new vistas. From that day forward, all nations would begin to receive the favor of God that Israel alone had enjoyed for centuries.

Peter obeyed and went to the house of Cornelius, who was a centurion who believed in the true God. He preached Jesus to him and his household. Miraculous results were immediate. Peter hadn't finished speaking when the Holy Spirit fell on the uncircumcised Cornelius and his household. That Gentiles could receive anything from the Lord was astonishing. Everyone was amazed. At once, the revelation of what God was doing dawned on Peter. He stated, "Ye know how that it is an unlawful thing for a man that is a Jew to keep company, or come unto one of another nation; but God hath showed me that I should not call any man common or unclean." With one short gospel message in the house of a Gentile, Peter had witnessed God performing a major shift. The dispensation of one nation's monopoly with God had come to an abrupt end. Things would never be the same again. God had completed a phase of work and again moved to an entirely new one.

However, just as expected, as news of the miracle among the Gentiles spread, there was mixed reaction. Some expressed anger that Peter shared the message of salvation with non-Jews. When Peter arrived in Jerusalem, certain Jewish Christians refused to have anything to do with him, condemning him for knowingly defiling himself by visiting and eating with uncircumcised men. In their minds, the report that the Gentiles received salvation was extremely suspect if it violated the Jewish law. They openly questioned why Peter was in the house of an uncircumcised man in violation of the law in the first place?

Peter patiently reviewed the complete matter before them all, from his vision on the roof to the Holy Spirit's infilling of Cornelius and his family. It became obvious to all those present that this was all orchestrated by God Himself and not of Peter's own doing. And although it was quite shocking to some, it was also obvious that the God of the Jews had extended His love to include uncircumcised Gentiles. But this was a fact that was very hard to swallow for those brought up under the law. Unwilling to give up their former status, Jewish Christians stubbornly held this practice of remaining separate, knowing full well that God no longer made a difference. The Apostle Peter had personally received the revelation of this change. But surprisingly, he also was unwilling to discontinue what God specifically had ordered him to stop.

As the leader of the church in Jerusalem, what influence he might have had exerted among those who would have serious struggles with this change. The excitement generated by the opening of the door of salvation to the Gentiles held unimagined possibilities. It holds true that those who are in the most danger of missing the fresh move of God are often the ones who were prominent in the last move. I believe Peter didn't confront this prejudice knowing that he would likely be persecuted and rejected for encouraging close contact with uncircumcised heathens. We see Peter later in Paul's letter to the Galatian church continuing in the same narrow-mindedness, neglecting to change his ways and neglecting to teach the Jews of the circumcision what God had revealed. Instead, he was still acting as if the Gentiles were unclean before God because of uncircumcision. He still refused to eat with them in the presence of other Jews.

Paul publicly confronted Peter about this, telling him that he was responsible for perpetuating division. Can you imagine Paul, a relative newcomer, rebuking Peter, a giant of the faith? Paul told him if you, being born a Jew, are not living according to the law, how dare you try to force the Gentiles to live by it? God himself had years earlier corrected Peter's theology. Why didn't he immediately throw down the old and embrace the new? Why was it necessary for Paul to chastise him on what he already knew? Whenever the move of God is ignored or neglected, another spirit comes on the scene taking many forms, such as pride and prejudice, even that of religion. While Peter's neglect did not stop the move of God, it was certainly a serious hindrance.

Scripture References:

Acts 10:14-15, 28   Galatians 2:12-14

Matthew 10:5-6; 15:24;16:18

CHAPTER 8
CHANGING WHAT GOD HATES

The time comes in each our lives when God refuses to tolerate our sick condition another minute. He then sets an appointment that cannot be postponed and shows up freshly scrubbed, scalpel in hand, ready to perform the operation. This time, however, the gentleness of His manner is gone and, though we may try to talk Him out of it for fear of the pain, there is no turning Him away from His will. The believer from that point on is in for a season of transition—a trying time during which there are more questions than answers, and in which profound change takes place.

What is God after? The one remaining feature in your life that continues to operate from fallen nature. He's no longer satisfied with correcting your errors. It's time to get rid of the source. Satan has already been cast out. But in the soul of mankind yet remains the rebellious imprint. With an infected mind, will and emotions, which comprise the soul, man cannot inherit the life of

God. In his soul, every man bears the two major treacherous sins of Adam, namely rebellion and independence. These are the sins that fly in the face of God. Both cling tenaciously to the deception that man and Satan can make a world without Him. It is soul life that was pieced together from the curse, natural life. God hates it. And spirit-led man hates it too. For it pretends to be life, but cannot hold a candle to the life God intended and holds in reserve for man.

After salvation, there remains in us a nature that masquerades as the real you. It is your soul, a major component of your existence, but not the real you. In it is housed your mind, will and emotions. It has an essential role in the shaping of our lives from childhood to adulthood. From it comes forth everything we have called life in this natural world. In it are our intelligence and feelings. In collaboration with the body, the soul of man developed the world system. Intelligence and feelings were the most prominent leaders in that system. The problem is that was not the way God originally designed us.

He designed us to be three parts—spirit, soul and body, not two. But when man sinned, his highest and brightest feature died. It was the one part of man that was an exact replica of God Almighty. The spirit is the highest part of our makeup. It is designed to rule the soul, and the soul is to rule the body. In order for us to function properly, God cannot continue to allow us to be governed by our natural intellect and feelings, which are soulish.

The scripture states that the Word of God divides between *soul and spirit.* That is the very thing God is doing to us, dividing between our soul and spirit. Man's mind, though qualified to translate many things into understandable portions, has never been God's medium of choice for direct communication with us. God designed us in His likeness; He is a spirit. That would make us spirits with souls and bodies. The mind, though useful in many areas in the natural physical world, becomes a serious encumbrance in the things of the spirit. Having grown accustomed to the limitations of the five senses, it cannot easily make the switch to the unlimited things of God. It must be removed from the lead position in our lives and repositioned into a position submissive to the reborn spirit of man.

Because believers are unaware that they have a spirit, they continue to do things in accordance with the soul. Trying to use their five senses and their minds can never be pleasing to the Lord. Simply put, with our spirits, we touch God, with our souls the intellectual world and with the body, we contact the physical world. He has been trying to move us into the life of the spirit. Therefore, everything must change. It's not just our actions that must change, but the source of those actions as well.

Up to this time, we have experienced His leniency and mercy in so many things. We have had no idea how stern He can be. The first few years of salvation are like a love affair with God. Whenever we cry, He immediately comes on the scene. He shows up when we're lonely, speaking to us in loving ways, attending to everything in a manner typical of a loving father. We in return tell everybody about this loving God who "catches you before you fall and answers you before you call." As long as we are children, we enjoy certain innocence, but in time, we must develop.

As immature children, we have had no idea of how much restraint it takes for our Father to continue to cater to our cries with full knowledge that they are coming from a part of our lives He hates. In addition, that is the very element the Father must destroy, though it has been an integral part of our lives for years. As David said in Psalm 51, we are born in sin and shaped in iniquity. Fully aware of how we are born and shaped, God loves us anyway. He lets the wheat and tares grow together in our lives, but at a certain point, He separates real life from its lookalike.

In our second birth, we are immediately changed where it counts, on the inside. All significant changes occur there first. As man looks on the outside, God is looking and has His attention on the heart—the center of our being. It is His place of residence and His chosen channel of communication with us. This part of man must be recognized openly and subsequently kept free of any interference. "Keep your heart with all diligence; for out of it are the issues of life."

In the fall of Adam, unfortunately, mankind chose knowledge over the things of God. He, in turn, received a world where secular knowledge is positioned above the revelation knowledge of God. In that choice was not just rebellion but also a satanically directed declaration of independence from God. Duped by a deceptive promise from Satan, they actually unplugged from the very source of life. But instead of the promised promotion to godlike status, man descended in a state of slavery, with Satan as his master. God's design was for man and God to work together to dominate the earth. Our interdependence upon each other would fuel the operation of the planet and be the springboard for possible exploration of places beyond earth. When man chose knowledge, he shut the door to revelation, that knowledge which is provided by the Spirit.

Eating of the very tree that God forbade was an act of rebellion against the Word of God and against the world of God. His creation works perfectly only in accordance with His Word. Disobey it or rebel against it and you will find yourself evicted from it. Rebellion is a serious enough sin, but along with rebellion comes another ominous setback, namely independence, a permanent disconnection from our life source. Independence is rooted in the erroneous exercise of man's soul. Made in three parts, man has individuality given to him by God through His creation. God formed man from the clay, which is of earth, and He breathed into his nostrils the breath of life, which is spirit life from God. Then man became a living soul. Not totally flesh as the animals, not totally spirit as the angels but in between the two, a living soul. The soul of man is the part that gives him the ability to choose. For he can either choose God as his leader or some other entity. Either way, his soul, which houses man's mind, his will and his emotions, is what makes him an individual.

After the curse, man's individuality lacked its major proponent, namely God. Relegated to a lower level of life, he would now make his living by the exercise of his mind and the labor of his body. His spirit had been put out of commission by sin; he was essentially dead to God and to the things of the Lord. Knowledge would no longer be provided as a benefit of being in the presence of the Lord, but it would have to be gained another way. Collected through the experiences of the body's five senses, knowledge could be categorized and filed away in the mind. This slow process of gathering knowledge would be repeated over and over again. As years turned into decades and decades into centuries, the mind of man rose to prominence now, being the highest of his faculties. In time, spiritual things were thought to be fantasy and unreal. Only what could be measured by the five senses is qualified to be called real. Anything else fell into the category of fantasy. Truth and believing ceased to be a part of each other. To this day, the separation continues.

Every major step of man since the fall has been independent from God. Man rejected God and set out to make his own way. The kingdoms of men and their vast stores of knowledge, their universities and governmental systems have been formed independently. It's that independence that God hates because it flies in the face of God to say, "I can do this on my own." Not realizing that the very structure of the universe is held together by God. Independence is a myth. Behind the scene, God lovingly keeps things together even though we are unaware He's the one doing it.

But as I stated, there comes a time when He will no longer tolerate this serious offense. We have made our own independent conclusions about how we got here. Some say man descended from apes. Our culture is filled with things manufactured without any approval from Him. The technology we have developed flies in the face of God's original intentions. From the time of the Tower of Babel to the Big Bang Theory, man's discoveries must cause quite a laugh in Heaven. God needs no jet to get around. His form of transportation is far beyond ours. If we had stayed connected to Him, by now we might have been getting around by the speed of light. Instead, we live in a world where our best and brightest minds largely ignore Him. It is quite appalling that one can go all day long in our universities or turn on the TV and there will be no mention of God.

In this, we have grown and been developed, and this is what we bring to God, a pitiful excuse for real life. What we call life is nowhere near His definition. Locked out of the spirit world, how could we even envision some of the things He routinely experiences every day? The soul life must be stripped away. All of the habits and routines of the natural world must go. It was shaped and formed in independence from God. He hates it with a passion. It is the god that we've placed before Him. But He's patient because He loves us. We have been able to use what was remaining after the curse to manufacture an entire world. It could never stand on its own, but we are raised to think it's OK. Really, to God it's obnoxious. The audacity of man to bring to God this manufactured reality and to expect Him to accept it. God is having none of it.

The Word of God divides between the soul and the spirit. In other words, God begins to separate what is manmade and what comes from God. We may have forgotten, but not God. There is a judgment coming; where all that is made from wrong substances will be burned. Even every work that we accomplish will be submitted to the fire. Whatever is not God inspired and God directed will be burned up.

When this happens to believers, it appears that God is being cruel. For the very thing they have called life—our routines, our habits, ways of doing things, even our whole lifestyle is being scrutinized and searched. At that point, there is no leniency and no mercy. The mercy is now in the fact that He is taking time to viciously tear away from you the disease that has been inherited from birth, which is doing internal damage. It's time for you to totally come out of any misconceptions about life.

God, without apology, attacks your wayward ways. When He shows up, we think He's there to comfort, when He's there to confront. No more time is allowed for drifting or even for other options. If you are committed to the kingdom, here is the price. Your life, the one you built through your natural mind. The one who is independent of God's principles. He wasn't consulted when you developed it, and consequently, it has been growing outside of His perfect will for your life.

GOD'S DIVINE PLAN FOR YOUR LIFE

This is also the time when God begins to direct your path concerning His divine plan for your life. We discover that before we were born, He knew us and predestinated us to accomplish a particular assignment. Now it's time to get to it. It's time to walk in the pre-ordained paths that God has set up for us. Immediately, the protection given for His permissive will is withdrawn. This is a dangerous time for those who are obstinate or those who ignore the voice of the Lord. Unknown to us, but known to God is the fact that there is a time when proceeding in the path that seems right but isn't leads to death.

God's mercy never runs out but man's time on this earth does. When God's protection is walked away from, whether intentionally or through ignorance, the result is the same—destruction. Trying to be something God didn't plan or attempting to do a work we weren't designed for causes heartbreaking destruction. This is the time when the scripture applies that states, "to whom much is given much is required." Having worked patiently with us throughout our lives, God can now expect us to walk in what we know. Like the children of Israel, He was happy to part the Red Sea and rid them of the Egyptian army, but years later when they came to the Jordan River, they had to step in before the Jordan would respond and back up.

Life as we know it is OK. It has its ups and downs. But to God, life as we know it is appalling. It was never meant to be. Man's mistake caused a world that suffers to this day from being outside of the designed blessings. Daniel saw the vision of man set up as an image composed of gold, silver, brass, iron and clay. But in the vision, he noticed that God's kingdom was not made of such material. Instead, it is a work by the hand of God that is destined to supplant it with God's kingdom. The Lord deliberately places us in that kingdom in position to cause his plan to come to pass.

Isn't this according to the pattern we have described? After living our lifetimes in natural life, having settled in for the long haul, having built around ourselves our own protective shield; it's just like God to come and change everything. Nothing of unregenerate man can remain, whether it is beautiful to the eyes or pleasant to the taste. Nothing can remain. I have a friend who stated, "When God is preparing you for the best, good is the enemy of best." In our finite minds, some things are good enough, but not to God. As we are a reflection of Him, we must ascend to the position He has designed for us. The thing is that during this stage of change, mercy is not the usual brand. This kind doesn't soothe; it hurts. The treatment is rough, but the cure requires that when He's finished, nothing of the natural remains. Those things that we lived with and played with are no longer allowed. Others looking on would say, "It doesn't take all that." But you know it does in order to rid you of anything resembling the natural world.

Jesus said, "Every branch in me that bears fruit he purges that it may bring forth more fruit." Pruning is a good analogy. The severe stripping that a farmer does to fruit-bearing trees seems to rape the tree of its beauty and branches. But what is being done is actually taking away anything that saps the nutrients. Then when the season for producing fruit returns, the tree is prepared to bring forth. Departure from dependence upon natural ability is the aim of this phase of change. God is our source, and He will have no other god before Him, even if it's us.

As old habits, routines and ways are abandoned, a new source begins to take up the newly vacated areas of our lives. Crucifixion, though unpleasant and arduous, was necessary. The natural life had to die and be taken away. God will not allow this pretender to stand alongside the life of the spirit. Natural life is filled with activity.People live their entire lives busy with affairs of life. But none of that activity has meaning except that which is directed and designed by him. Because God is alive, we have purpose, His purpose. Take Him out of the world and what's the point?

Scripture References:

Daniel 5	Ephesians 2:10
Hebrews 4:12	John 4:24; 15
Psalm 51	Proverbs 4:23
Romans 8:30	I Corinthians 3:13-15
Samuel 16:25	I Thessalonians 5:23

CHAPTER 9
CHANGED TO REIGN

Scriptures reveal to us exactly what God thinks about man. The scripture states, "If any man be in Christ he is a new creature; old things are passed away; behold all things are become new." They also state, "they which receive the abundance of grace and of the gift of righteousness shall reign in life by one, Jesus Christ." God's Word here reveals His thoughts. He's now looking at born again man as an entirely new species. He is also expecting those who have received His grace and the gift of righteousness to reign in this life or to use their God-given authority. These things are in the mind of God and revealed through His spoken Word.

Now, if God is thinking this way, is He simply having positive thoughts toward mankind or is He expressing through Paul another significant change for mankind? To me, it is obvious there has been a significant change in God's dealing with man. Those who fail to pick up on it are in danger of again being left behind. In God's mind, we are new creatures who are in authority in the earth. Why would He reveal to us His thoughts? Why inspire Paul to write these glorious statements about man?

God cannot help but speak the truth, and He never wastes time on fantasy. We, therefore, have only to agree with Him on this in order to realize this tremendous blessing in our lives. The scriptures imply that once man hears the good news, he must agree and begin to act on what he has heard in order to start the process of manifestation. He said we are a new species and that our former state has passed away. He said that we are to reign in life. When God says something, we must agree and respond. In faith, we will begin to speak the same thing and begin to meditate on what He said until it becomes a part of our consciousness--until God Himself gives us further revelation on it.

Those who are sensitive to the changes that God makes fully understand that if we are to please Him, we can never return to our former state. We can no longer think or act as if we are "just human." And we can no longer think or act as if we are not in authority in this life. Those who return, fulfill the scripture that says, "No man having put his hand to the plow and looking back is fit for the kingdom of God." Those who expect to live in victory in this life as believers do not have the option of looking back or returning to the former state. The Lord said, "Now the just shall live by faith; but if any man draw back my soul shall have no pleasure in him."

In Adam, we lost everything. But Jesus recovered all that was lost in the fall. What Satan did in Adam cannot be more powerful than what Almighty God did in Jesus. If this is true, why do people continue to act as if we are still under the curse? Let us begin to walk in the benefits of what Jesus did. His accomplishments dwarf Satan's work. He came to destroy the works of the devil. Did Jesus accomplish what He came to do, or was Satan able somehow to escape? The very notion would indeed be ludicrous since we know that Jesus said He possessed all power. As definite as sin and death are to every human experience, ruling in this life should be much more definite. As real as funerals and the grave should likewise be the reality of our power over death and the grave. We all realize we have to be much more assertive in this area.

Jesus' recovery over all that was lost in the fall relates directly to the year of Jubilee. It occurred a year after seven Sabbath years in the 50th year. It was known as the *acceptable year*; a year when every Israelite who had been sold into slavery was released and every individual who had lost property was given back their land. What a generous and merciful statute! If an Israelite who had fallen upon hard times could make it to the fiftieth year, he could be restored. This would mean that the person was now at peace or made whole.

The Jewish concept of peace or *shalom* was essentially the condition where nothing is missing and nothing broken. This gives peace an entirely new meaning. Anyone studying the Bible knows that anything of significance that God did for Israel was a pattern of what He planned to do for every believer. If He set up a year for restoration of everything lost for them, there would surely be an even greater event for born again believers. When Jesus began His ministry, He read from the Book of Isaiah chapter sixty-one. He read the portion, which states, "he has anointed me... to preach the acceptable year of the Lord." And He stated, "this day this scripture is fulfilled in your ears." Jesus was declaring to His chosen people that just as there was an acceptable year for the misfortunate among Israel, there would be an acceptable year of release and restoration for the whole world. In ancient times, once the sacrifice was made to atone for the sins of the people, the trumpet would sound signaling the year of Jubilee.

In like manner, when Jesus was crucified and was raised from the dead, He told His disciples to go into the entire world and preach the good news, sounding the trumpet of jubilee. When the angels startled the shepherds with their singing, they left the message that peace was on earth and good will toward men. Shalom was now on earth, the recovering of all that was lost in the fall. As a direct result, great miracles, too numerous to record, occurred in His ministry. And after His resurrection, signs and wonders occurred among His followers and were promised to all that believe. If we can but believe that the year of Jubilee has long since arrived, we can begin to experience the wonderful benefits.

How often have we heard people say, "I'm just human."? They really think they're being humble, when actually they're speaking against what God has said. And how often have we heard people throw up their hands and say, "Whatever!" As if nothing can be done about their situation, so they're submitting to conditions that are unacceptable. The tragedy here is that this kind of thinking can last and continue to be perpetuated over an individual's lifetime. Thus, relegating well-intentioned Christians and those around them to lives of unexplained defeat. Not because of sins committed per se, but for being out of step with God.

Scripture References:

Hebrews 10:38   Luke 2:14; 9:62

Matthew 28:18   Romans 5:17

II Corinthians 5:21   I John 3:8

CHAPTER 10
ABANDONING INEFFECTIVE PRAYERS

I believe I can fully understand the reason there is not more answered prayer. Over the centuries, prayer has remained an exercise for the religious with little more serious credence given to it in the natural world than that given to poetry or mythology. All are nice to read but have very little real effectiveness to cause real change. Jesus was very definite and very serious about prayer. He called it the cure for "fainting" or falling apart. Paul said, don't be anxious or worried about anything, but pray about everything. People are praying the way they were taught by the elders or their parents or teachers to pray. They meant well, but far too often, they didn't know how to pray effectively either.

Prayer must of necessity submit to the process of change as well. We cannot consider it too sacred a practice to submit our prayers to the same scrutiny we are submitting our very relationship with God. It is evident that many prayers, too many prayers, are just not getting any detectable response from the Lord. They seem to be, for the most part, a religious exercise for the devout or desperate cries by those searching for a last hope miracle. Or, religious words designed to comfort the hearers. Both are accompanied by the same response from God, silence. But the participants rise up to feel better that they have at least made an attempt toward divine assistance.

AN INTOLERABLE SITUATION

We have allowed a largely intolerable situation to exist far too long in our prayer lives. Unanswered prayers and cruel responses to prayer should never be acceptable to believers. I have heard devout people say that they prayed for patience and God gave them cancer. Just imagine what that did to their prospects for divine healing. If God gives you cancer, who can take it away? Wouldn't the doctor who's working to get rid of it be found working against God? And, wouldn't our efforts to rid ourselves of the disease be defined as disobedience? God doesn't give cancer, but many are convinced otherwise. Because God is always present with us in trouble, we have misconstrued His presence to mean His approval. God is present, mainly for the purpose of delivering us. "Many are the afflictions of the righteous, but the Lord delivers him out of them all." Jesus cleared up this issue when He stated, "Everyone who asks receives...

Which of you, if his son asks for bread, will give him a stone? Or if he asks for a fish, will give him a snake? If you then, though you are evil, know how to give good gifts to your children, how much more will your father in heaven give good gifts to those who ask him!"

When we are not receiving desired results from praying, we are truly in a fix. Prayer is not just our request line to God, but also our entire line of communication with Him. It doesn't take much wisdom to recognize the enemy's strategy to infiltrate this vital lifeline. If the enemy is successful in causing frustration in our prayers, our confidence in God's faithfulness will wane. We will begin to attribute to God what the enemy has sent. Jesus stated for the eternal record the heavenly Father's position on it. We must now get busy and enforce the written Word in our lives. Search the scriptures first before we pray to make sure we are asking in line with His will. Then, I John 5:14 states, "This is the confidence we have in him, that, if we ask anything according to his will he hears us. And if we know that he hears us, whatsoever we ask, we know that we have the petition that we desired of him." We'll have to spend time meditating on this scripture to see what God is saying to each of us personally in order to get the full impact of it.

EFFECTIVE PRAYER

According to Jesus, prayers that are prayed hoping for

an answer "someday" in the future are largely ineffective. He stated in Mark 11:24, "What things soever ye desire, when you pray, believe that ye receive them, and ye shall have them." When we pray, we are to believe that we receive. What a total change from the way we are accustomed to praying! When we ask, we need to stretch our faith to believe we are receiving. That's God's design for prayer now. When we are more comfortable with receiving when we ask, we will be more in line with the words of Jesus on praying effectively.

Prayer has evolved over the years with our revelation of what happened at the resurrection of Jesus Christ from the dead. Many very powerful transformations happened there that we're just finding out about. And as we find out about them, we must believe what God said. The problem with many Christians is that we are praying prayers that God cannot respond to. He cannot respond because we are spending time asking for what is already ours. As we dig deeper into the Word of God, we find that some statements are **facts** that have already occurred and others are **promises** requiring our obedient actions for manifestation. Every believer needs to search the scriptures and find out what God has already provided and, by faith, arm themselves with those facts. They are not negotiable. Then we can cooperate with God by taking a stand to bring them to pass in our lives.

THE GREAT ACCOMPLISHMENTS AVAILABLE TO US

Through the great sacrifice of Jesus, marvelous feats were accomplished for the benefit of all of mankind. Accomplishments so wonderful that we find it difficult to conceive in our minds that they are actually true, but according to God's Word, they are. John, the great writer of the Book of Revelation, wrote that through Jesus we have been raised to the position of **kings and priests**. Paul said that we actually have been *raised up together, and made to sit together in heavenly places*. Both statements speak of an elevation of mankind to a new position of authority that relatively few of us have exercised. Here are some things that have already taken place:

1. We have been **delivered** from the power (authority) of darkness (the devil)—Colossians 1:13

2. We have already been **translated** into the kingdom—Colossians 1:13; Christ has **redeemed** us- Galatians 3:13, Colossians 1:14

3. We are already **reconciled** (brought into favor and harmony) with God—II Corinthians 5:21

4. We have been given **all spiritual blessings**-Ephesians 1:3; God has given us **all things that**

5. **pertain to life and godliness**- II Peter 1:3; We have been **raised up and seated** with Christ in the heavenly realm—Ephesians 2:6

6. We have been **predestined, called, justified and glorified**—Romans 8:29,30

7. We are **a new species** (creation) on earth, **the sons of God**—II Corinthians 5:17, I John 3:2

These are things that have already been undertaken. They are facts, not promises. To pray for any of these benefits is to ask the Lord for what is already ours. Acknowledging what things the Lord has already done is cooperating with Him. Acknowledging what He has done also exercises faith, as we confess with our mouths what His Word attests has been accomplished. Who can continue with religious exercises when we have access to such an array of benefits and blessings? We must take hold of these and say what the Word says. *I am redeemed. I am raised up and seated together with Christ in heavenly places. I walk in the favor of God Almighty.*

Prayers must acknowledge the accomplishments of God. This is the way God sees things now. And He has inspired His New Testament writers to record them. If we don't see things the way God sees them, we aren't just lagging behind; we are deceived. The manner and method of our praying must change and catch up with all that Jesus has purchased for us. Otherwise, we once again begin to lag behind the fresh move of God. Resist the tendency to pray as usual. Pray God's Word and notice the difference.

Scripture References:

Colossians 1:13-14

Ephesians 1:3; 2:6

Galatians 3:13

Luke 18:1

Mark 11:24

Matthew 7:8-10

Psalms 34:19

Revelations 1:6

Romans 8:29-30

II Corinthians 5:17, 21

John 3:2; 5:14

II Peter 1:3

CHAPTER 11
LIVING WHERE GOD WAS

The old song *Footprints* has a nice little message about faithfully following the footprints of Jesus. Although the song is sweet, following footprints is no longer acceptable in this life. It means we're too far behind the Lord. We must now follow and be led by His voice. We cannot afford any longer to be that distant from the Lord. After a long period of disappointing results in my ministry, I asked a pastor friend what was wrong. To my thinking, we ministers were serious in our walk with the Lord. We tithed and lived a sanctified and separated lifestyle. Why were we so far behind other groups in progressing toward a better life in God? The pastor said something that really stuck with me. He said, "Our problem is... we're where God was."

Apparently, from what he was able to judge, God had moved on and unknowingly we had gotten stuck on past issues. Our main biblical arguments were regarding the Godhead (Trinity), baptism, outward apparel, excessive makeup and jewelry and whether women should be allowed to preach. Immediately, I could see his point. Too much time was being wasted on things of the past. The serious question should have been asked, *What is God supporting now?* We would have benefitted from a thorough house cleaning, throwing out all old debris. But that would have meant organizational suicide. Any change from what the founder taught would be looked upon as *worldliness* and immediately rejected by the ever-vigilant old guard.

These were pastors and ministers who were so steeped in denominational doctrine that any change was condemned as a first class ticket to hell. Every year during the ministerial segment of the convocation, behind closed doors these ministers angrily argued against allowing any compromise. Each convention ended pretty much as it began, without any change, though everyone knew it was desperately needed. Instead, the arguments continued, providing plenty of fodder for more time-consuming debate, which lead nowhere. Every few years someone would restart the campaign to return to the roots of our beliefs, purging out all the *outward worldliness* and returning to the *old landmark*.

I always thought that, although these efforts were well meaning and the people were sincere, no more meaningful manifestations of God occurred or could be detected. Being "where God was" meant walking in a system of beliefs that had a strong anointing in the past, but now only a residue remained. Practices and methods of the past that from all reports did bring awesome and miraculous results, now have only a memory of what used to be. Like the law of old, those that live by the law should continue to follow its many practices with a full understanding that these ordinances can keep you quite occupied with that form of godliness. They will provide you with a holy standard of a past dispensation. But the fresh anointing is missing and cannot be experienced by those who are where God was. Yesterday's practices don't result in yesterday's anointing but stagnation.

THE FUTILE ATTEMPT TO BE RIGHT WITH GOD

For the most part, I've found that all who strive to please God by certain outward practices such as outward apparel, or strict codes of conduct have totally missed the concept of righteousness. They are essentially working to achieve something already given as a gift. Although this may seem an insignificant misjudgment, it results in disqualification from the greater blessings of the Lord. If righteousness could be achieved by any work of man, Jesus would not have had to suffer and die. But righteousness or right standing with God is a gift. It cannot be earned. It is not the result of doing right things but will result in doing things right.

Righteousness must be received by faith. "For with the heart man believes unto righteousness." It must be taken and grasped by faith; claiming the unseen work of God rather than achieving an outward conformity. The scripture states, "But to him that worketh not, but believeth on him that justifieth the ungodly, his faith is counted for righteousness." Grasping the concept of our right standing with God will eradicate much of the self-defeating guilt that is ever-present in those who lag behind in the things of God. Trying to achieve what was already theirs was the problem the Jews stumbled over after Jesus paid the price for their sins. Having become accustomed to works of law, they yet tried to establish their own righteousness. They consciously refused to submit themselves to live as though righteousness were a gift. They thought they still had to earn it with works; thereby missing God and confining their entire group to a life of always striving, but never quite reaching perfection. The scripture also states, "And all things are of God, who hath reconciled us to himself by Jesus Christ." Through Jesus' sacrifice, we are already in God's favor. We must believe that and act accordingly. Looking at our many faults, mistakes and outright sins, some cannot bring themselves to believe that through Jesus, we are *right with God*. But that's recognizing the work of the enemy in our lives instead of believing the Word of God. Paul said concerning righteousness, "Where sin abounded, grace did much more abound."

In our present circumstances, certain endeavors require a level of strength that cannot be demonstrated while any trace of guilt or self-condemnation remains. While these blessing blockers remain, we cannot take the stand necessary to uproot the entrenched enemy of our blessings. We must know absolutely that we have right standing or we will never even attempt to possess what the scriptures declare is ours for the taking. Righteousness protects the vital organs of our lives. Paul called it the breastplate of righteousness.

When we were able to accept our right standing with God, knowing that in Jesus we are right now *right* with God, we can begin to reign. When the realization hits home that we don't have to wait until we get to Heaven to know that we're right with God, we will excel here on earth. I have always believed that just as we accepted that we were born sinners into this world, we should much more readily accept that we were born again righteous.

TRYING TO REVIVE
WHAT GOD IS FINISHED WITH

I heard a famous preacher say, "If you're going to walk with God, keep your bags packed." When God finishes with something, He moves on. If we're walking with Him, we must move on too. Any time spent on that which God is finished with is wasted time and becomes a dangerous derailment from the track of our divine purpose.

We must be very wary of allegiances to people and groups. Commitments to them can render us unable or unwilling to make changes when it becomes apparent that God has shifted. The desire and need to be liked seems harmless, but in our walk with God, it can be paralyzing. It keeps some individuals bound with fear to depart from what they know has developed into a form of godliness denying the power. The love of the praises of men, which John warned of, then becomes stronger than the love of the praise of God.

As I travel around the country, it is apparent that in some areas it was never God's intention to establish a church. The work was meant only to be a short-lived work, but someone decided to build an edifice for whatever the reason. Maybe a misplaced sense of duty or responsibility was the culprit. As a result, the fresh anointing is now gone, but of habit, the people continue.

FAULTY LEADERSHIP

God warned Israel against faulty human leadership. It was never His will for them to be ruled by a king. He wanted to be their king. That way, they would never have to suffer the indignities resulting from the personality flaws and egotistical agendas of human rule. It is well known that power corrupts and absolute power corrupts absolutely. The tendency of otherwise decent normal human beings is toward abuse upon the realization that people must bow to their authority.

Throughout history, men and women alike have shown themselves unworthy of rule over the lives of others. God told Israel, "the king will take your sons for his chariots and your daughters to be cooks." He knew the inclination of man in power. Exalting his attributes covering his mistakes, rulers have made a real mess of things. Their subjects, destined to live in the circumstances created by the sins and/or the wisdom of the leadership. God never wanted us to live with our "teeth on edge" because our leaders had eaten sour grapes. But that is the dilemma. How often have we uncovered facts hidden by leadership in order to save face, which cost the lives of hundreds and thousands of soldiers and innocent individuals? It is indeed a hideous set of circumstances to have to suffer and die for someone else's irresponsibility, whether a king or ordinary person.

So it was with Israel starting with Saul. The Books of the Kings and Chronicles list both good and evil kings. Under the God-fearing kings, Israel prospered, but under the evil ones, they lost precious ground. Eventually, the evil kings prevailed to the point Israel was taken captive never to return to their original glory. Centuries later, when Jesus came on the scene, they had been passed from the hand of one conqueror to another. He found them under the rule of the Romans, serving Pharisaical leadership with outdated laws. The masses of them neither knew their God nor understood His ways. Because of faulty leadership, they were totally out of step with God.

When leaders rule, the common man must yet maintain personal communication with God. So if the leadership veers, they will remain on track. The story of the three Hebrew boys perfectly confirms this. Although in bondage under the rule of the pagan king Nebuchadnezzar, these young men refused to be misdirected from following God. Under threat of the frightening death of being burned alive in a furnace, they stood their ground. Wouldn't it be wonderful if we all were the same?

SAUL'S COVER-UP

The prophet Samuel mourned when the Lord told him He had rejected Saul from being king over Israel. He wept bitterly and had difficulty accepting the change. But God had shifted and taken the anointing from Saul and planned to place it upon David. From that moment on, Saul should have willingly abdicated his position or should have been forcibly removed. But because two people who were aware concealed this major change, Saul remained in power. The prophet Samuel did not disclose what he knew to the people. He kept it between himself and Saul. The cold, naked truth was that Saul was no longer king.

From the moment God rejected him, it didn't' matter that he wore the crown and sat on the throne. In effect, he was no longer king to the one who mattered most, God. However, at Saul's desperate pleading, Samuel pretended all was well by accompanying the king to the sacrifice. It is always a mistake to allow ourselves to be influenced by emotion when we are aware that God has made his final decision. Accordingly, this would soon prove to be a disaster in the making. The sight of the prophet accompanying the king to sacrifice was designed to spare Saul public embarrassment. The peaceful presence of the prophet implied that God was in agreement when just the opposite was true. Samuel's mere presence caused people to tremble because he had God's favor and his backing. The prophet was the one person with more authority than the king. Actually, it was Samuel's anointing with oil that gave the king his position. Why he was suddenly afraid of Saul is more than a little puzzling. The fact that the king was honored instead of openly exposed made Samuel complicit in the cover-up. The populous of Israel were none the wiser.

Like sheep, they dutifully obeyed the orders of a man disqualified to be king over God's chosen people. Saul was spared open embarrassment, but the people of Israel would soon suffer defeat and slaughter as a result of following a king God had essentially dethroned. When God decided Saul's reign was ended, at that point everything in the kingdom should have responded to God's move. But it didn't. Knowing that his anointing had been replaced with an evil spirit, Saul frantically seized every opportunity to retain power. Everything took a downward turn from that point on. The Philistines invaded the land with their champion, the monstrous Goliath, striking fear into the hearts of everyone who saw him. Every major decision from Saul from that point on would not be from a person ruling by divine right but from a demon-oppressed imposter. The coming years would find Saul using his considerable kingly resources and his well-trained handpicked soldiers in a campaign to track down and kill David. Unknown to his many loyal subjects, the very one they sought to kill was the one God had newly anointed to be their king. What could have and should have been openly exposed in one bold moment years earlier by the prophet Samuel, instead lasted for years, until Saul's untimely death at the hand of the Philistines. The attempt to revive what God is finished with inevitably results in years of time wasted and lives lost.

THE RESURRECTION CHANGED EVERYTHING

When it was obvious that the law was no longer in effect, all those who had profited from the status and the business the law generated resisted the change. Priests, merchants, shepherds, Scribes, and Pharisees were all no longer functioning parts in the fresh move of God. In one stroke, God had withdrawn from generations of history and commerce. Immediately after the death of Jesus on the cross and His resurrection, everything changed. Mankind was now reconciled to God.

The words of the angels to the shepherds on the night of Jesus' birth had been prophetic. Peace was now on Earth, and God's extremely good will was now flowing toward men. The mess that Adam made was now corrected. Everything lost was returned and everything stolen was recovered. Man was reconciled back into harmony with God. The captives were liberated. But there was one problem. None but a small band of men knew about it. No doubt, the very next day after the resurrection, there were those who came to offer lambs for sacrifice at the temple altar, unaware that the Lamb of God had already taken away the sins of the whole world.

The priests returned to resume their duties without any understanding that the High Priest after the order of Melchisedec had already begun His ministry in the heavenly tabernacle. They were, in essence, unemployed and the work they continued to perform was essentially meaningless. God had fulfilled His period of dwelling behind the veil of the temple. He had finished an entire dispensation, and the very people intimately involved in it were largely yet in the dark.

The temple curtain had been torn to signify His departure from there to take up His new residence in man. Miracles were happening, signs and wonders were occurring, but the greatest miracle of all had escaped their view. In fact, it would be years before word got out about what the Lord had accomplished in Jesus' death.

Not until Paul wrote his epistles did the world get an idea of what God had done in Jesus. Paul spoke of an elevation of the status of man in the eyes of God that was powerful. We actually began to see ourselves as a new species of being in the Earth. He recorded that the complete former state of man had passed away and that all things had become new. It is sad and unfortunate that we should miss the wonderful workings of God, especially when the very quality of our lives depends on them.

Scripture References:

Ephesians 6:14

Hebrews 6:20

John 12:43

Timothy 3:5

I Samuel 8:10-13; 15:35; 16:4

II Corinthians 5:17-18

Romans 4:5,15; 5:17,20; 10:3, 9

CHAPTER 12
WHEN YOUR ANOINTING CHANGES

Moreover the Philistines had yet war again with Israel; and David went down, and his servants with him, and fought against the Philistines: and David waxed faint. And Ishbibenob, which was of the sons of the giant, the weight of whose spear weighed three hundred shekels of brass in weight, he being girded with a new sword, thought to have slain David. But Abishai the son of Zeruiah succoured him, and smote the Philistine, and killed him. Then the men of David sware unto him, saying, Thou shalt go no more out with us to battle, that thou quench not the light of Israel—II Samuel 21:15-17 (King James Version).

In this passage, David apparently expected the same protection he experienced when he first faced Goliath, but to his surprise, it was no longer present. As Israel fought against the Philistine army, another giant, Isbebenob, came forth. David engaged him in battle but apparently became too weak to continue. All of Israel held its collective breath in horror as their beloved leader collapsed before the giant. Only by the grace of God was he spared as Abishai, son to Zeruiah, came to his rescue. Years before, everyone had heard of what he had done to Goliath. The tale of the shepherd boy who killed the giant with a stone was by now a highly publicized story well on its way to becoming folklore.

King David had gone into battle with the usual confidence, unaware that something was missing. Something so special that without it he could not have victory. It was the anointing God gives to accomplish His will. David nearly lost everything trying to operate in an anointing he no longer possessed. Could he have forgotten the words of the prophet Samuel? That the sole purpose of his rise to prominence was to replace Saul as king of Israel? As a young man, he operated as a warrior, and the Lord prospered him to defeat all his foes. But when he became king, that anointing was no longer his to walk in. He would now have to operate as a king with different responsibilities and a different authority. The responsibilities of ruling God's people was now priority. It was now more important for him to rule as *the light of Israel* than to fight as a soldier. The temptation to conquer another giant would have to be resisted, for it was simply not to be. The task of hand-to-hand combat, though necessary in battle, was now given to others.

Nowadays, it can be quite disturbing to any believer to attempt to accomplish something, which God has routinely supported in the past, only to find that support suddenly missing. But as wonderful as they are to operate in, anointings change with the will of God and with His ultimate plan for our lives. What we start out with often changes in accordance with God's intended outcome for us. As the scripture states, "And we know that all things work together for good to them that love God, to them who are the called according to his purpose." Everything must be yielded to His purposes in order to qualify for His goodness. "We are his workmanship...taking paths which he prepared ahead of time that we should walk in." Only in the paths God has ordained for us will we find His support. And it appears that the longer we walk with God, the less room there is for deviation from that path.

In the beginning, God will work with us in a *permissive* will with some room for mistakes and blunders. But as we mature and our time grows shorter in this life, His divine will is less tolerating. A noted Bible teacher once stated that he was a pastor for twelve years before he found out that his real ministry was to be a traveling teacher of the Word. During his time, no one knew anything about a teaching ministry. Pastors and evangelists were the only full-time callings recognized as legitimate. However, in the course of performing pastoral duties, he found himself experiencing a deep uneasiness in his spirit. He constantly felt like he was out of place.

Finally, after some time seeking God, the Lord spoke and told him, "You know, I never called you to pastor." What a shock, that after twelve years of serving as a pastor he found that he was on the wrong path. Reluctantly, he began to hold meetings teaching the Word. His meetings became so successful he left the pastorate never to return. Denominational expectations and roles, as well as organizational requirements, can obscure the real purpose of God in our lives. It's up to each individual to discover the will of God for their lives. Sometimes the withholding of the anointing and support is the signal that change is imminent.

We may indeed start the day in one role and end it in an entirely different one. Jesus is a great example of this. He started out a great prophet, preacher and miracle worker, healing the sick and raising the dead. But when it was time for His real purpose to be fulfilled, that of dying on the cross, it was a difficult transition. In the garden of Gethsemane, we see Him struggling with His true purpose. He had recently ridden through Jerusalem like a triumphant king. The common people were unrestrained in adoration because of His mighty acts. He had not long ago raised Lazarus from being four days in the grave. Caught up in the moment, the people stripped branches from the trees and cried out, "Hosanna to the son of David. Blessed is he that cometh in the name of the Lord." It was a celebration unlike any other. The entire city was moved. This was the hour of His triumph among the people. When the Pharisees tried to stop the celebration, Jesus said, "if these should hold their peace the stones would immediately cry out." But this high point was to be immediately followed by a new low.

As His crucifixion hour approached, intense prayer was needed for Him to say, "Not my will, but thine be done." When He resigned Himself to do His Father's will, the power to accomplish it was immediately made available to Him. He then was no longer in turmoil over it. The courage to endure the torturous crucifixion and the agonizing death that followed became His. In His death, He gained much more than in His entire life on earth.

In order to accomplish the death of the cross, it was necessary for Him to be wounded and bruised. This could only be accomplished if the protective ring around His life were lifted. When the soldiers came to take him, they said, "We are looking for Jesus of Nazareth." He said, "I am he," and they fell to the ground at His very words. This is proof that His power was yet with Him. Then He relinquished His authority and spoke with less force. It was only then that they were able to take Him. Some who followed Him were not able to handle the change of anointing. Peter was ready to fight, emboldened by a misguided expectation that God would surely rescue His son. He brandished a sword and severed the ear of the high priest's guard. Jesus, having resigned Himself to lay down His life, healed the soldier. Totally confused that Jesus was not defending Himself, Peter withered from his bold defense of the Lord, and moments later denied he ever knew him.

Scripture References:

Ephesians 2:10 Amplified

John 18:6

Luke 19:40; 22:42

Matthew 21

Romans 8:28

II Samuel 21:15-17

CONCLUSION THE FINAL SHIFT

The Apostle Paul had a real struggle with his flesh. He cried out "O wretched man that I am who shall deliver me from the body of this death." This is quite a shocking statement from this highly revered man of God. It appears that his flesh had a mind of its own. When he wanted to do good, he reported that evil was present. The evil that he didn't want to do was asserting a disturbing influence. His struggle was so terrible he thought of himself as *wretched* because of the alarming presence of sinful inclination still at work in his life. His writing about his struggle is strangely comforting to those of us who have experienced the same alarming symptoms. Thank God, through his struggle he locates the doorway of escape.

I believe that unwittingly, Paul may have been selected to be the vessel chosen by God to usher in the final major change for man. The anguish he was experiencing was like the travailing experienced by women just prior to birth. He was in transition from allowing the things of the natural world, its feelings and thinking, to have control over his life. It was time for the believers to depart from the former way of living. The time of the spirit had come. This was a wrestling for who would lead man, the old fleshly nature or the new indwelling Holy Spirit. But in the eighth chapter of Romans, we see the breakthrough into a new realm that up to that time had never been discovered. It was the breakthrough to the realm of the spirit.

Far too long ago in the fall of Adam, the realm of spirit had faded. Because of our inability to see that realm with natural eyesight, it seemed unreal. But through the prophet Ezekiel God promised mankind, "I will put my spirit in you and you shall live." His promise was kept on the day of Pentecost when His Spirit was poured out and at once became accessible to all men. Jesus told of the Spirit of Truth coming from the Father to lead us into all truth. He said we would be "born again" of that spirit, opening up to fallen man the restoration of a forgotten realm.

Many centuries ago, we lost track of our spiritual heritage, the fact that we were made in God's likeness. God is an Spirit. To be made in His likeness is to be made of the same substance. But we long since lost almost all spiritual attributes. God called us "dead," unable to communicate with Him on a spiritual level. And as a consequence, unable to be like Him. His task through the centuries was to bring us back to our origin. Coming to the realm of the spirit may be considered new to some, but in reality it is a return to our beloved homeland. *Born in sin* was not our original state. Our origin was godliness from the beginning. As each believer is reborn by faith, he or she clears the last major hurdle.

In the spirit, things are much different than in the natural. Total faith or trust in God is the key to unlocking every door. Love is prized above all things, even above the exercising of the awesome gifts of the spirit, with its miracles, healings and prophecies. In the realm of the spirit, giving is called "sowing" or planting seed. There is also the promise of reaping the harvest from the seed planted. There, things unseen to the natural eyes are more real than those that are seen. It is known there that the unseen realm is the "mother" of the seen. It is common knowledge to the spirit realm that "the worlds were framed by the Word of God, and things which are seen were not made of things which do appear." Words spoken in faith rule the day. They have the power to modify any physical thing. They are spoken with much reverence for their power. None are spoken without purpose.

Following the spirit qualifies each believer as a greatly loved son of God and a joint heir with Jesus. Living in the spirit is life and peace here on earth. Paul's revelation of what it means to walk after the spirit and not after the dictates of the flesh freed our lives forever. Walking in the spirit is the place where the love of God is experienced most strongly. Paul recorded, "we are more than conquerors through him that loved us." He also stated that nothing "shall be able to separate us from the love of God which is in Christ Jesus."

Paul describes the place we have come to in our rebirth. He states, "But you have come right up into Mount Sion, to the city of the living God, the heavenly Jerusalem, and to the gathering of countless happy angels: and to the church, composed of all those registered in heaven; and to God who is Judge of all; and to the spirits of the redeemed in heaven, already made perfect; and to Jesus himself, who has brought us his wonderful new agreement; and to the sprinkled blood which graciously forgives instead of crying out for vengeance as the blood of Abel did."

STAYING IN STEP WITH GOD

Before God does anything significant, he always tells His people. Always. They don't always pay attention or take to heart what He's saying. But God always lets us know. Adam was forewarned that there would be a great change the very day he ate of the forbidden fruit. Noah knew for more than a century that the flood was coming. Abraham knew long beforehand that his offspring would be captive slaves in Egypt and that they would ultimately be delivered. Moses was very aware of two opposite scenarios. If Israel obeyed God, he was told of the blessings that would be theirs, if not they would be cursed. They disobeyed, and the history of Israel is filled with the fulfillment of the terrible consequences they endured.

In the New Testament, Jesus told us that the Holy Spirit would show us things to come, which he does constantly. Unfortunately, we don't take advantage of this benefit. The many cares of this life, business pressures and responsibilities drown out the "still small voice" of the Lord. As a result, many have become dull of hearing when it comes to the things of God. That makes this period an extremely dangerous time for God's people. Because if we are missing what He is saying to keep us protected from coming tragedies, how can we expect not to be assaulted by an enemy who walks as a roaring lion seeking opportunities to destroy?

Sad to say, many have already experienced terrible tragedy that could have been avoided. God doesn't foretell us of future dangers for us to live in fear of impending doom. He tells us in time for us to either prepare ourselves or to change it through prayer and intercession. Isaiah told Hezekiah the king who was sick at the time, "Get your house in order you're going to die." Hezekiah didn't do either one. He didn't get his house in order or make final arrangements for his passing. And he didn't die. What happened? He turned his face to the wall and prayed. Before the prophet could get out of the palace, God told him to return to the king and tell him he had fifteen more years. It is now obvious to us that God was not telling him what was inevitable, but He was telling him what would happen if things continued as they were. Prayer and intercession change and affect everything. "The fervent effectual prayer of the righteous availeth much."

A woman once told me a dream she had of her son drowning, which tragically took place just as she had dreamed. She relayed this story to let me know she was gifted in the prophetic. I was appalled at what a grievous and preventable tragedy this was. God was not telling her so she would experience the terrible loss of her son. But so she could be aware of coming danger and begin to intercede to change it. "Oh what peace we often forfeit, oh what needless pain we bear. All because we do not carry everything to God in prayer." The words to that old song are so true.

Often when I find myself in a quandary about what to do, time with the Lord is all that is required. There is, however, a peculiar thing that happens in every one of those times with Him. After giving me time to quiet my hurried thoughts about the problems, He always takes me back to something He already told me. It's like finding solid ground in the middle of sinking sand. What

He said always prepares me for what's coming in the future. God will always give you words today to guide you through what's unfolding in your tomorrow. We would do well to give "more earnest heed to the things we've heard lest at any time we should let them slip." We are living in a time now when we must be able to trace everything we're doing to something the Lord said. Otherwise, we could be far off track. His Word assures us that what we are doing is His will.

We are admonished in to "strip off and throw aside every encumbrance (unnecessary weight) ... and let us run with patient endurance and steady and active persistence the appointed course of the race that is set before us." This is a deliberate action we take--stripping off and throwing aside everything that we detect is hindering us from our appointed course. We realize when there's a hindrance. Conditions change, the flow of anointing ceases and a coolness replaces the fire of the Holy Ghost. Anyone experiencing such conditions should immediately take action.

Resist being rocked to sleep because your walk with God is at stake. God told the church of the Laodiceans, "I wish you were hot or cold. Because you are lukewarm and neither hot nor cold, I will spit you out of my mouth." All denominational affiliations, clubs, relationships, habits and routines, everything must come under scrutiny when we have discovered our assigned course to run. Anything and anyone diluting our resolve, dampening our enthusiasm, destroying our focus or blocking our forward motion must be confronted. Just as in the time of Moses, when the cloud moves, we must follow the cloud. In that cloud is everything we live for and everything we need.

Scripture Reference

Romans 7:24; 8	Hebrews 2:1; 11:3; 12:1, 22-24
Ezekiel 37	I Peter 5:8
John 4:24; 16:13	Isaiah 38
Amos 3:7	Deuteronomy 28
James 5:16	Revelations 3:15-16

BIOGRAPHICAL SKETCH

Al Gee was born in Miami, Florida, the third of seven children born to Allious and Mable Gee. Growing up in a devout Christian family, he was taught daily to believe God for the impossible. Time and again his family relied on faith in God for basic necessities, which produced miraculous results that would forever shape his life. Also having personally experienced divine healing from childhood disease, he developed a deep and ongoing relationship with God.

He attended Long Island University in New York, graduating with a degree in Sociology. After graduation, he worked for the Atomic Energy Commission as a Management Specialist and completed graduate courses in Public Administration at St. Johns University. Al was set to pursue a career in government when in 1976, after four years in the Commission, he acknowledged his calling to the ministry. That acknowledgment drastically changed his life and took him far away from the New York area.

That year the church leadership assigned him the task of starting a new church in Omaha, Nebraska. Immediately, he resigned his position at the Commission to accept his first ministry assignment. Building on street evangelism, weekly Bible study, radio broadcasts and intercessory prayer, he established Faith Deliverance Church. While in Omaha, he also met and married his wife Debby and proudly fathered their three children: Yahtta, Christian, and Brittney. After serving twenty years as a pastor, which included the completion of a required 5-year training program, he was consecrated to the office of Bishop in 1996.

Having completed his work in Nebraska, Bishop Gee returned to New York and in 1999, accepted a new role as the Director of the Higher Education Opportunity Program at Long Island University. He also founded Faith Fellowship Ministries, a teaching ministry on Long Island, to equip believers with the same revelation knowledge that transformed his life and ministry. With years of experience as a pastor, evangelist, convention speaker, teacher and university administrator, Al Gee has committed his life to empower believers and congregations throughout the world with keys to powerful living and insights to life-changing kingdom principles. The Gee family presently resides in Durham, North Carolina.